# Making Connections

## Building Community and Gender Dialogue in Secondary Schools

Nancy Beardall
Stephen Bergman
Janet Surrey

CONTRIBUTING AUTHORS
Gayle Burnett
Lisa Sjostrom

esr
EDUCATORS FOR SOCIAL RESPONSIBILITY

*Making Connections: Building Community and Gender Dialogue in Secondary Schools*
by Nancy Beardall, Stephen Bergman, and Janet Surrey


esr

**EDUCATORS** FOR **SOCIAL RESPONSIBILITY**

Educators for Social Responsibility
23 Garden St.
Cambridge, MA 02138
www.esrnational.org



Cover and book design by Schwadesign, Inc. (www.schwadesign.com)
Book Production by Jessica Phillips



10 9 8 7 6 5 4 3 2

Printed in the United States of America

ISBN 10: 0-942349-23-7

ISBN 13: 978-0-942349-23-8

# DEDICATION

This work is dedicated to Nancy Goodman (1950-2002), whose generosity of spirit and passionate commitment to young people will always be remembered and lives on in this work.

*Making Connections* is also dedicated to our children:

Katie Surrey-Bergman
Victoria Beardall Gwin
Darren Beardall Gwin

# ACKNOWLEDGMENTS

We are deeply grateful to the director of the Wellesley Centers for Women, Susan Bailey, and former Stone Center directors Carolyn Swift and Cynthia Garcia Cole, for their support and encouragement.

We also thank with great appreciation the Gender Relations Study Group, which met from 1998 to 2000 at the Atrium School, Watertown, MA. Cate Dooley, Rebecca Koch, Connie Henry, Mary Murray Meade, Marsha Mirkin, Richard Perry, Carol Watson Phillips, Georgia Sassen, Pamela Seigle, Lynn Stinson, and Katie Wheeler all contributed enormously to the development of this work.

Our colleagues at the Jean Baker Miller Training Institute, Jean Baker Miller, Irene Stiver, Judith Jordan, Linda Hartling, Maureen Walker, Wendy Rosen, Amy Banks, Yvonne Jenkins, and Natalie Eldredge have been a source of great inspiration and theoretical wisdom. In addition, Jan Putnam and Peggy McIntosh have been important supporters.

We'd like to thank the Gender Task Force, of Newton, MA, which consisted of a dedicated group of parents, teachers, and administrators who initially brought Janet Surrey and Stephen Bergman, from the Gender Relations Project at the Stone Center, of the Wellesley Centers for Women, to speak to their group. It was there that the collaborative effort among Janet Surrey, Stephen Bergman, and Nancy Beardall began.

We want to thank Nancy DiMella, Newton's Health Coordinator, for her support in bringing Making Connections to the Newton Middle Schools.

We'd especially like to thank the teachers and counselors who piloted *Making Connections* in the Newton Middle Schools: Carley Gibson from Oak Hill, Linda Wolf, Elizabeth Messina, Sam Schneider, and Sharon Finelli from Brown, Sharon Milinsky from Bigelow, and Rachel Morales from Day. We also appreciate the efforts of Jamie Moore, and Dan Simone from Newton North High School and of dance colleagues Pamela Newton and Deborah Smulian-Siegel.

We'd like to acknowledge Lesley University graduate interns for their input and energy: Valerie Blanc, Gabrielle Salvatore, Jennifer Heney, Heidi Feinstein, Kim Robles, Nicole Davis, Krista Neilson, Aparna Rao, Brie Anderson-Feldman, Sivan Burkstein, Regan Mosher Rudolf, and Krysten Carter.

We'd like to express our gratitude to the Frank A. Day Middle School administrators Paul Stein, Joe Bannen, and Sheryl Bono for their confidence and support.

We'd especially like to thank Barbara Carlson, who was one of Nancy Beardall's mentors when she began her teaching career and who helped brainstorm with us the best ways to communicate the teaching process in the *Making Connections* curriculum, and to Norma Canner, who encouraged Nancy to bring the expressive arts to the public schools.

Thank you to the staff at Educators for Social Responsibility (ESR) and especially Audra Longert for her commitment and support of this project.

Finally, our heartfelt thank-you to our students, whose spirit and voices brought this work to life.

# TABLE OF CONTENTS

*To facilitators of the Making Connections curriculum:*

After numerous discussions with teachers and students, the authors feel it would be useful to make aspects of the curriculum more explicit to better support youth, particularly GBLT students, feel more included and affirmed, and thus, more able to voice their own experiences.

It has always been our intention that the curriculum be inclusive, safe and challenging of gender and sexual stereotypes. Our goal is to give all students the opportunity to be authentic and connected. We recommend that the leader/facilitator be very explicit in affirming the range of sexual and gender identities while appreciating the reality that students are at different levels of clarity regarding sexual and gender development and different degrees of comfort in speaking about these.

At every point in the curriculum, the facilitator must be sensitive, affirming and welcoming of differences. Here are a few possible suggestions for facilitation depending on the particular group and the developmental level of the students:

• In the beginning of Lesson 3 when students are asked to form same gender groups, the leader should ask students what it means to make a gender choice as this may not be easy or clear for all students. Have students reflect in writing what this choice means to them and what it might mean to others?

• When students are asked to reflect on same gender relationships, the leader should explicitly state that same gender relationships do not have the same meaning for everyone.

• In a preventative way, predict potential invisibilities and misunderstanding or targeting of GLBT students to highlight the pervasiveness and destructiveness of heterosexism and homophobia.

# INTRODUCTION:
## Fundamental Frameworks of *Making Connections*

This curriculum is designed to teach middle and high school students a language and tools for creating connections, building community, and addressing disconnections in same-gender and cross-gender relationships. The purpose is to create an optimal relational and cultural context for growth in which disconnections can be named, challenged, and transformed in order to build healthier connection.

The program has been piloted with many hundreds of secondary school students, ages ten to eighteen, for whom it has resulted in increased relational competence and enhanced learning environments. *Making Connections* moves competence in connection—relational competence—from the background to the foreground of education. A sense of connection in the classroom and to the school, combined with a strong sense of community, creates the optimal context for academic achievement for all students.

The Fundamental Frameworks of *Making Connections*

Connection

1. Learning about Connection — This curriculum is based on recognizing the centrality of connection in young people's lives and learning. Teaching the essential concepts and language of healthy connection is one of its primary objectives.
2. Learning through Connection — The curriculum utilizes relational connection as the primary context of learning and pedagogy. Dyads, small groups, role-plays, and dialogue are examples of fundamental interactive and experiential practices that support and foster mutual growth and connection.
3. Learning in Connection — The underlying objective of this curriculum is to empower young people to speak their authentic experience, and to learn through the process of engagement and interchange. Teachers/leaders need to support this goal through the expression of trust and faith in the process of interactive learning. Constructively acknowledging cultural differences in defining and practicing connection can build greater mutual awareness and understanding.

Working with Gender

1. Promoting Engagement — This curriculum is based on the belief that healthy engagement within and across gender groups is a valuable practice in building healthy relationships and healthy classroom and school

communities. It assumes that while unaddressed gender differences may create division or separation between and among students, this divide can be utilized and redirected to support healthy connection.

2. Beyond Gender Stereotypes — It is essential to distinguish between the reinforcement of gender stereotypes and a respectful inquiry or open engagement with differences. Because this can be a difficult and emotionally laden process, educators may avoid focusing on gender as an aspect of diversity. This curriculum provides a process for working with gender as it impacts relationships.

3. Engaging Gender Differences — Gender is one aspect of diversity within any community; it intersects with other sources of diversity. This curriculum highlights gender as one important doorway to difference. All differences can create separation or stratification within a group, but conversely, they may also be engaged to build connection, community, and the larger "we."

4. Gender and Cultural Diversity — Constructively acknowledging cultural differences in gender styles, roles, and relationships can build greater mutual awareness and understanding.

# CONNECTION

## The Importance of Connection

Human beings of all ages desire and thrive in good connection. Research and theory on infant and adolescent development suggests that participation in authentic, responsive, and mutual connections with others is central to healthy psychological growth and development.[1] Although the importance of connection may seem obvious, social and academic norms in the United States still focus on self-development as the primary goal. The culture often urges students to succeed and compete at any cost, without regard for their impact or influence on others.

Relationships are seen as background supports to individual development or relegated to private spheres of friendship or social groups. Connections are rarely the focus of attention at school, and are rarely considered a primary component of the learning process. Addressing disconnections that arise across group differences is not often accomplished constructively. Adolescent culture is highly stratified by popularity, often with stereotypical or dominant cultural ideals defining what is "cool," "popular," "in," or "out." Life at school is often experienced as a zero-sum game, an either-or endeavor, resulting in academic and social winners or losers, popular kids or "nerds," "jocks" or "geeks."

Individualist and stratified norms typically pervade the classroom. Students are usually measured and graded, praised and criticized for *individual* performance. Exceptions to this rule are most likely found in extracurricular activities where, in order to win the game, stage the play, or perform a choreographed dance or a piece of orchestral music, *group* effort is indispensable. Except in the very early grades, there tends to be little *curricular* emphasis placed on teaching and practicing the skills necessary for creating and maintaining connections with others, and for working constructively with disconnections as they occur, both in the classroom and throughout the whole school environment.

Recent studies have shown that when middle- and high-school students feel connected to school, they are less likely to engage in risky, unhealthy behaviors.[2] They are less likely to use alcohol and drugs, less likely to become pregnant, and less likely to engage in violent or deviant behavior. Moreover, when they feel connected to school they also report higher levels of emotional well-being and respond better to efforts to improve their academic performance. A curriculum that fosters healthy connection can be useful not only for a particular classroom or grade, but for the larger school community as well. In a safe and connected school environment, optimal learning takes place, and classroom management is easier and more effective. Research has shown that when friendship groups within a school are more integrated by gender and by race, students as a whole experience a greater sense of connection to school.[3] In addition, supporting understanding through dialogue around differences, teachers can foster healthy relationships and a sense of connection within and outside school. Promoting friendships between boys and girls contributes to the overall health of individuals and the community as a whole.

## Qualities of Healthy Connection

The theoretical framework for this work is based on the Stone Center Relational-Cultural Theory, originating at the Stone Center, Wellesley College.[4] This model emphasizes the basic human yearning for connection and the growth potential inherent in building authentic and responsive connections with others. This perspective broadens the focus from individual development to the quality of connections and disconnections between and among people. Central to healthy growth is relational development: the nature of a person's psychological health can be observed through the qualities of the connections he or she creates and sustains with others.[5] The health of the community can also be observed through this lens.

For example, after a positive encounter with another person or within a healthy group, each of the participants comes away with five "good things": a feeling of increased zest or energy, more knowledge of both self and other, a greater sense of worth, a greater ability to take action, and a desire for more connection. These are essential qualities of well-being and motivation for life and learning. In a hurtful or less than optimal interaction with another person or group, each person goes away with the opposite qualities: less energy, less knowledge of self or other, diminished sense of worth, less ability to take action, and a movement toward isolation.[6] These are qualities of immobilization, loss of motivation, and emotional and intellectual constriction. In school situations, this experience can lead to lowered achievement, painful social isolation, and the potential development of depression, substance abuse, eating disorders, and other symptoms of psychological stress evident in adolescents.

**QUALITIES OF HEALTHY CONNECTION**

**Healthy relationships and healthy communities often exhibit these characteristics:**

| | |
|---|---|
| RESPECT | An attitude of careful interest, appreciation, and regard |
| ENGAGEMENT | Sustained presence and involvement in the moment |
| ZEST | Positive energy and joyfulness in interaction or shared activity |
| ATTENTION | A focus on what is happening both in oneself and in the relationship; being present and interested |
| EMPATHY | The ability to understand and resonate with another's feelings, experience, or perspective; the capacity to "put oneself in another's shoes" |
| AUTHENTICITY | The quality of being oneself and speaking one's truth |
| DIVERSITY | The ability to respect, value, and learn from differences even when they create conflict and disconnection |
| MUTUALITY | Shared participation in a relationship; genuine interaction between persons; energetic responsiveness on behalf of all participants |
| EMPOWERMENT | The capacity to act, resulting in an increased sense of personal and collective power and well-being |
| MUTUAL EMPOWERMENT | Enhancement and empowerment of both or all participants through the connection |

| | |
|---|---|
| DIALOGUE | The process of attending, listening, and responding with awareness of the other as an individual and of the relationship as a whole; the intention is to understand and expand awareness for all participants |

## The Concept of the "We"

At the heart of this model is the concept of the "We." In addition to self and other, I and you, there is a third element in human experience called the "We," "the relationship," or "the connection." The healthy "We" is open, growing, and inclusive—fostering engagement with others of different views and cultures. Individuals interacting in such a "We" develop and grow in a matrix of healthy mutuality. This curriculum promotes an "and" model: I *and* you *and* we. Diversity thrives in a healthy "We." If a person is part of a healthy "We," he or she feels *more* him- or herself, more able to interact in productive ways with others, and more able to work energetically and effectively at school.

The Stone Center Relational-Cultural model has been applied by Drs. Surrey and Bergman in their work with couples and with men and women in various institutional settings, particularly educational settings at all levels—from preschool to postgraduate. This work has been published in the book *We Have to Talk: Healing Dialogues between Women and Men*, which can serve as a primary sourcebook for the theory and background of this curriculum.[7]

*Making Connections* evolved over many years as a collaborative effort with Nancy Beardall, and through the merging of the creative process, relational cultural theory and a pedagogy that reflects both. Ms. Beardall, educator, dance/movement therapist and wellness and prevention counselor in the Newton, Massachusetts public schools, has developed and designed the curriculum *Creating a Peaceable School: Confronting Intolerance and Bullying*.[8] Her experience in curriculum design and implementation and her commitment to building caring and connected communities has facilitated the application of the theory of the "We" in the *Making Connections* curriculum.

## The Classroom "We" and the Connected School "We"

When students are authentically connected, the entire classroom is affected positively.[9] However, when a classroom is marked by discord, division, or disengagement based on race, gender, popularity, or other stratifying forces, students cannot grow or learn as well, particularly when these disconnections cannot be named, addressed, or transformed. When a classroom culture values and is organized around building healthy connections and transforming disconnections, people can work through challenges that arise over schoolwork, class management, disrespectful behavior, discipline, etc. When a classroom is not connected, each of these issues becomes a problem, taking time and energy from learning and impacting the school community. The crucial issue is the quality and movement of connection. This curriculum is designed to help create the qualities of healthy connection that support a classroom or group, students, and teachers, and help them feel safe at school and encourage them to produce their best work. As one student observed, "It takes everybody working together to build the class 'We.' It is what we all want and like. It's a sense of belonging."

When a teacher says, "I've got a really good class" or "a really 'difficult' class," he or she is often talking about the degree and quality of connection or disconnection in the room. Research is confirming the validity of what most teachers experience every day: the relational climate in a school has a direct effect on students' ability to concentrate, learn, and achieve.[10] A healthy "connected classroom" has a strong sense of "We" within which all individuals are positively affected and influenced. This spirit of connection exists not only in the classroom, but influences interactions throughout the school—at sports events, in the cafeteria, at recess, during extracurricular activities, and even on the bus ride home. Students feel they belong, feel connected to each other and to caring adults, and feel respected for who they are. They feel they can participate in ways that foster other students' well-being and growth and their own. Building and caring for the "We" then becomes a crucial component of individual identity and self-regard for students. See Appendix II for additional strategies that foster connection to school for administrators and parents.

**Ten Strategies that Foster Connection to School**

*For Teachers*

1. **Help students** get to know each other's (and your) strengths.
2. **Involve students** in planning, problem solving, identifying issues, and assessing curriculum in the classroom.
3. **Promote cooperation over competition**. Post everyone's best work. Offer opportunities for the class to work together to help everyone achieve their level of excellence.
4. **Build a strong relationship** with each student.
5. **Convey attentiveness** to students and excitement about learning through nonverbal gestures.
6. **Involve all students** in chores and responsibilities in the classroom.
7. **Integrate concepts of discipline and respect** for classmates throughout instruction.
8. **Give students more say** in what they will learn.
9. **Involve students** in developing the criteria by which their work will be assessed and provide guidelines so they clearly understand what's expected of them.

10. **Use first person plural** (we, us, let's) when presenting classroom activities.

* *Used with permission from the Center for Adolescent Health and Development, University of Minnesota. Based on material published in "Protective Schools: Linking Drug Abuse Prevention with Student Success," by Kris Bosworth, PhD. Smith Initiatives for Prevention and Education, College of Education, The University of Arizona, Tucson, AZ.*

# WORKING WITH GENDER

## The Hidden Curriculum of Gender: The Gender Climate

Gender grouping is a common root of disconnection in schools, yet it is rarely, if ever, identified as such. *Making Connections* allows educators to find ways to talk about or work with gender differences respectfully. On the one hand, there is a tendency to avoid the discussion altogether, saying, "There are no real differences between girls and boys. For example, some of the most assertive students in my class are girls." On the other hand, there is a tendency to resort to limiting stereotypes: "Boys will be boys," or "It's just a girl thing. They'll get over it." In many schools, destructive experiences of gender separation, stereotyping, and shaming are in full operation, but are rarely acknowledged, named, or discussed in open, constructive ways as aspects of gender relations. It is difficult to find a way to work with issues of difference without being criticized or quickly accused of stereotyping. In doing this work, it is essential to keep the focus on the more silent, marginalized voices within each gender group. Because this balance is so difficult to achieve, educators often shy away from doing gender work. This curriculum offers a way to work both comfortably and effectively with gender and diversity. We recognize that this work requires careful attentiveness, trust in the process, and the humility and commitment to "stay in the learning" for the sake of growing healthy connections.

The Gender Climate refers to the quality of gender relations throughout a school. It is often not a temperate climate, but tends toward extremes. In many schools, it is not a climate that promotes health, happiness, or diversity. In general, two separate relational cultures exist almost from the beginning of school. If you enter a preschool class, you often see gender separation—boys interacting with boys and girls interacting with girls. Thus, with few exceptions, boys learn about relationships from boys, and girls learn about relationships from girls. From about age five, cross-gender contact diminishes even further. For the next approximately five years, boys and girls travel different relational paths.[11] Many have little authentic contact with each other, little chance to grow and understand each other. This is the gender rift of early childhood.[12] It is not until middle school, with the challenge of adolescent development and the influence of hormones that many boys and girls try to connect. By then, they have often become mysteries to each other. In high school, they start to have powerful and formative experiences relating across the gender divide, but often still lack the information, skills, and education needed to build healthy connections.

This gender separation can build to a crescendo in late elementary and early middle school, with the separation or even segregation of the genders (often rigidly enforced by kids), cross-gender teasing, shaming and devaluing, playful and not-so-playful power and control battles (who owns the playground, the girls versus the boys), and enforced sexualization of boy-girl relationships. Homophobia plays out in these years as part of this bullying and shaming. Often those who cross the gender line are called "gay" or "lesbian," even before kids know what these words mean. If boys and girls try to sustain cross-gender friendships and socialize outside of school, they may *insist* that their parents tell no one about it. Cultural differences in gender roles may also create difficulties and misunderstandings.

These years of elementary- and early middle-school segregation we might call "The Years of Missed Chances"—lost opportunities for cross-gender relational understanding and growth. In the so-called "normal" pathways of child and adolescent development, we can see the seeds of psychological suffering and relational disturbances.[13] It is important to address the idea that what is considered normal development during this period may not be optimal development. We have found that *the dominant voice is not the majority voice*. That is, the dominant "boy voice" or "girl voice" in a group, the voice that sets the group standard, may not be the voice of the majority of girls or the majority of boys. At heart, most students want mutual, authentic, caring connections. This curriculum gives these nondominant voices a chance to be heard, to help the whole group build resistance to the rigid norms of the dominant voice, and to steer the conversation toward diversity, pluralism, and growth-fostering connection.

Gender separation and the tyranny of the dominant voice affect every aspect of students' lives—not only who they hang out with, but also what interests they pursue, their aspirations and life goals, and their ability to pay attention and participate in class as well as to achieve academically. This negative school climate can be called "The Hidden Curriculum" because although it is usually present in various degrees, it is rarely addressed explicitly. The purpose of this curriculum is to bring the hidden into light, to make the implicit explicit, and to help heal the conflict and wounding that result from the shaming across the gender gap.

Gender socialization and heterosexualization of gender relations are often at the root of the homophobia and gay-bashing that can be so prevalent in middle school. Pervasive images of male dominance in teen music and popular culture, as well as precocious sexual behavior among preteens, also have an impact on gender relationships.

In middle school, when boys and girls do try to connect, they often hold stereotypical and unrealistic views of each other. In cross-gender settings, boys often "play" to other boys, promoting the dominant male cultural view and saying things to girls and about girls they would never say if they were alone with a girl or away from their male peer group. In their initial attempts at flirting, some girls in groups also taunt and shame boys.

Gender differences also appear in boys' and girls' different learning styles. Girls tend to like working with other girls in groups, while boys may prefer and accomplish more working by themselves. For both girls and boys, however, certain sports teams, student government, and especially community service projects offer an opportunity to work together productively.

Gender differences can affect the multiple ways of learning and knowing. When teachers are not aware of different learning styles, the differences can negatively affect the quality of the learning environment. When teachers and students understand the differences, these differences can add to everyone's learning experience. For example, the fact that boys call out more often than girls can be dealt with, and that girls bring skills that make task groups function better can be addressed. Mixed-gender groups may, in fact, be able to build on the different strengths of both boys and girls so that everyone's learning is enhanced.

## Background Thinking about Gender

Gender dialogues inevitably bring out crucial issues for both boys and girls. They are encapsulated simply in the examples that follow. Although the responses come from middle-school students, the themes resonate into high school and beyond.

"What do you most want the other gender to understand about you?"

Samples of boys' answers are:

> "Don't believe how I act; it's not who I am."
>
> "We act like jerks around you because we're nervous."
>
> "Who I am inside."
>
> "Please see my heart."

The message the boys are sending is that there is a part of them that is hidden—the "nice guy," "caring," "heart side," "who I really am." Listening to boys, we hear their desire for connection, a desire many expressed easily until the age of three or four when cultural messages begin to silence their relational voice. This curriculum provides opportunities for boys to connect with girls and with each other and foster the boys' conscious awareness of their relational needs. Boys' friendships are often tied to *doing* things together, like sports or computers, with a lot of physical activity and a dash of aggression. The theme of their friendships is, in general, "*Who's up, who's down.*"

Examples of the seventh-grade girls' answers to the same question:

"What do you most want the other gender to understand about you?"

> "We want to be taken seriously."

"We're not Barbie dolls and anorexic blondes."

"We're your equal; we're as good as you."

"We go home at night and cry into our pillows."

"We're as smart and tough as you—but we just bruise easily."

"Our emotions are real, it's not just PMS."

The girls are saying that they have a sense of being treated as "less than," and are making a declaration of their strengths, standing up for themselves with a defensive tone. They are assertively telling the boys' that they can hold their own. They are protesting the boys' assumptions that girls "just want to be with guys" or are "just there for you to go out with." There is a suggestion of sadness and hurt behind these protests. Listening to the girls, we are moved by how misunderstood they can feel: objectified, devalued, angry, and hurt. Some already feel the cultural labeling of many of their strengths as weaknesses, the pathologizing of these strengths as "oversensitive," "wimpy," or "too emotional." They make it clear that such evaluations have a real impact and can hurt deeply.

Girls say that friendships are the most important things in their lives, yet they feel that their relationships can be unstable and unpredictable—they can be lost in a second. Emotional closeness, talking, and helping are valued most. Much of what goes on in girl-girl friendships can be put in terms of "*Who's in, who's out*," and the recognition of the fluidity and precariousness of this kind of evaluation.

Members of both genders have the same underlying desire: to be seen and accepted for who they are, and to make real and positive connections with the other gender. They sense that school could be a lot easier and happier for them, and they could achieve more, if they could better understand the other gender and the relational dynamics going on around them.

For students who have bridged this gender divide, the issues of friendship and dating are more immediate. These students are open to moving toward a deeper dialogue, which can mobilize energy to work together around issues of stereotyping, media literacy, violence prevention, date rape, and substance abuse prevention. For high-school students, this curriculum can promote collaborative teen action in these important aspects of their life.

## Gender Stereotypes

We clearly do not suggest that all girls or all boys are alike; there is marvelous diversity within as well as across gender groups. That said, there are differences in the ways that male and female development is constructed in the dominant culture that result in *overall* group differences between boys and girls. From early on, children are presented with distinct "girl" and "boy" cultures, even within their own cultural groups. There are "girl" clapping games, "girl" clothes, "girl" hairstyles, "girl" colors, even "girl language and intonation." Likewise, there are "boy style" games, "boy" expressions, "boy" posturing, and so forth. Not every girl conforms to gender norms, of course, nor does every boy; but research suggests that a certain number of girls do gravitate to "girl culture," just as a certain number of boys gravitate to "boy culture."

Stereotyping can lead to idealization of members of the other gender: girls can get typecast as princesses, boys as romantic heroes. Either way, whether girls or boys are put down due to stereotypes—or put up on a pedestal—they are not being seen for who they are as individuals.

Those students who deviate or differ from gender norms do not escape their influence. In fact, these students, especially, can be shamed, with lifelong consequences. For instance, consider the girl who is a genius at math or excels at football or the boy who writes poetry. The fact that gender norms exist will strongly influence their personal and relational growth. These students often feel greatly supported by this curriculum.

Cultural norms may deviate from dominant gender norms which can create difficulties and misunderstandings. The curriculum encourages deeper understanding of culture as it impacts gender.

## Relational Stereotypes

Students are shaped by limiting and controlling images of how they are supposed to act in same- and cross-gender relationships. From the moment they are born, they pick up on these relational images from the media, the culture at large, and from examples set by adults, older siblings, and peers in their lives. Images of girls relating to girls, boys to boys, girls to boys, women to men—these images can structure their actual relationships, too often in ways that limit the possibility for authentic connection with others.

For example, traditional relational stereotypes suggest that one way boys can successfully connect is to act "cool," as if they don't care about connection. Girls, on the other hand, are encouraged to maintain connection at any cost. Many adolescents go to great lengths to avoid or minimize disconnections from their friends, and suffer terribly at the inevitable adolescent disconnections and relational violations they encounter. This curriculum enables teachers and leaders to see beyond what look like the typical responses to small slights or disconnections and understand that they may matter greatly in students' development into adulthood.

## Theories of the Origin of Gender Differences

It is far beyond the scope of this curriculum to critically analyze all the research on gender differences. However, it is clear that no one model of the origin of gender differences will suffice. We certainly appreciate the biological factors which underlie gender differences, particularly the new research on gender differences in brain structure and brain chemistry and hormonal impact on brain development at every stage of life. It is also clear that individual, familial, group, and cultural factors deeply influence and shape gender development. The work of this curriculum rests on an appreciation of the multidimensionality and the plasticity of gender differences for individuals and cultures. Many differences may be biologically based, but are profoundly shaped by family and culture. And there is always room for growth and enlargement of gender possibilities. We hope to encourage an inquiring, open-minded, and growth-promoting approach to the dialogue on differences.

# THE IMPACT OF CULTURE ON *MAKING CONNECTIONS*

A rich and broad definition of diversity includes differences of all kinds. Gender, race, culture, sexual orientation, socioeconomic status, religious beliefs, different abilities, learning styles, and personality profiles are all elements of diversity. Along with gender, culture has a large impact on identity and on behavioral rules for relationships with others. For that reason, we want to take a closer look at culture and its impact on connection.

While a mainstream culture can be identified within the United States, there are as many cultural values in operation here as there are cultures represented. Understanding how we differ from each other is the first step toward making connections across these differences. In this section, we describe some of the differences in cultural rules, roles, and expectations, making no relative value judgments about them. Each of us has preferences that have been greatly influenced by our cultural norms; this curriculum is designed to facilitate the exploration of these differences. Our aim is not to teach students which values or beliefs are correct, but to help them discover which values and beliefs are correct for them, and at the same time to broaden their understanding and connection to others.

For many educators, multicultural education encompasses the study of language, learning styles, foods, lifestyle, holidays, and other visible elements of culture. Anthropologist Edward T. Hall found that culture establishes our behavioral preferences for the dimensions of communication, the use and meaning of space and time, power, the development and maintenance of our relationships, and much, much more. He labeled cultures *high context* or *low context* based on their behavioral expectations within these dimensions; we will use that framework in the next section.

## Cultural Context

Hall's research concluded that high-context cultures, in general, have a more collective orientation, while low-context cultures are more focused on the individual. For high-context people, space is collective. Houses often have one common room that is shared by everyone, with family bedrooms connected to that main room. In these family compounds, grandparents, parents, and children—multiple generations—live together. In everyday interactions, people from high-context cultures tend to need less physical space between themselves and the person with whom they are communicating.

Within low-context cultures, space tends to be viewed as individual property. "You're in my space" and "Don't invade my space" are expressions of this concept. There is an intense need for separate space, with the amount of physical space often viewed as a sign of status or wealth. At work, executives and high-level managers enjoy their own offices, with the head of an organization occupying the largest. Families live in separate homes, apart from grandparents, and children sleep in their own bedrooms, apart from parents.

High-context cultures tend to be hierarchical, with roles within the family clearly prescribed. The success of the family, even of the nation, is dependent upon how well the members engage in their roles. If they all understand their place and fulfill their duties, then success is guaranteed. While a given member may perform with excellence, it is often considered his or her duty. Any rewards that are received because of that performance will be given privately and quietly.

Low-context cultures tend to value individual choice and accomplishment. In low-context cultures, students are singled out for exceptionally good or poor performance. Star players on sports teams are treated lavishly, given large salaries, and promotion celebrations.

Storytelling is an art in high-context cultures. Members rely on subtle nuance in communications and will often tell long and descriptive stories to make their point. The underlying assumption is that listeners will extract the information that is important to them. In many high-context cultures, interrupting the speaker in a conversation to add a point or share a similar concern is unthinkable. In low-context cultures, however, people tend to communicate in the fastest and most efficient way. "Stick to the facts" and "Get to the point" are examples of the low-context orientation to quick and efficient communication.

Hall posits that we are not consciously aware of much of our cultural knowledge; some of it was learned when we were very young, before the acquisition of language. This cultural knowledge impacts our expectations and assumptions regarding behavior. When those expectations are not met, misunderstanding and disconnection often result. This is less of an issue in culturally homogeneous student groups because everyone understands the unwritten rules and assumptions governing behavior. Students are free to build relationships while exploring the process of building those relationships according to their cultural norms. However, in groups with students from diverse cultural backgrounds, each operating with his own cultural assumptions and behavioral expectations, the process of building and exploring relationships will take on the new dimension of cultural difference.

## Cultural Views of Connection

The concept of connection differs from one culture to the next. In mainstream American culture (which Hall defines as low-context), we perceive ourselves as individuals creating connection with one another. In higher-context* cultures (African, Asian, Hispanic, and Native American, for example) the perception of the self is defined by the person's connection to the community.

For example, in Japan, a child is not called by name, but is often referred to as "a student in a certain school" or "a boy or girl from a particular family."[14] Even family members are not referred to by name, but by their relative position in the family. Aunt Sara (low-context U.S. reference) becomes Third Auntie on my father's side of the family (high-context Japanese reference). Without the community and a clear place in it, the high-context sense of identity is deeply undermined.

In high-context cultures, members are so connected to the community, tribe, or family that most decisions and actions are based on the nature of that connection. Making decisions without placing the well-being of the community first is outside of the norm. For students from high-context cultures, the idea that you have to work to create connections that do not automatically extend to you as a member of a group is a lesson they often learn through difficult experience.

Many high-context, black Caribbean students new to the United States and living in New York City expressed surprise and deep hurt at the exclusion they encountered here based upon their race. The pervading sentiment was that in their originating culture race was not a factor in determining inclusion. These students identified themselves as Trinidadian, Jamaican, etc.; prior to coming to the United States, their race was not a critical part of their identity. (Different characteristics in their originating cultures influenced their inclusion: economic status, for example.)

Facing exclusion is difficult for any student, regardless of the characteristic that prompts it. Students who have faced repeated isolation and exclusion will come to mistrust the environments that allow such exclusion to take place. In a

* While certain cultures will be referred to as high- or low-context (as labeled by Hall), it is essential to note that every memeber of a cultural group will mirror that culture's context. Individuals who have had extenxive exposure to cultures with different contexts and/or who have lived in highly urban and rural enviroments may exhibit behavioral differences that are very different from that of their original culture.

classroom working toward connection, sensitivity to these students' experience will be essential.

## Cultural Differences in the Classroom

In his book *Beyond Culture*, Hall tells us that our culture also has a strong influence on our memory and thinking. For example, teachers in the Middle East focus on verbal memory because it is believed to be critical that students are able to recall large amounts of information. Reference books and materials are used infrequently because so much information is memorized. Students coming to the United States are surprised by what appear to them to be lower expectations. Other differences have potentially greater impact on student life.

The typical American classroom, with its focus on individual behavior and achievement, may unintentionally foster a sense of isolation in very high-context students. For example, in many high-context cultures (particularly in rural areas) a student experiencing difficulty with a lesson would be coached and supported by his classmates and the teacher. The whole class would not move on to another lesson until each student was ready.

The standard American classroom is very different. Students spend a great deal of time working individually and are responsible for their own work. High-context students entering an American classroom from another culture may experience a sense of isolation and exclusion, not only due to any existing language or racial differences, but also to the perceived lack of classroom support (connection) their cultural orientation leads them to expect.

The *Making Connections* classroom is designed to allow students to share their thoughts and feelings so they can build healthy connections. In the first few sessions, facilitated conversations may lead students from mainstream American culture to disclose thoughts and feelings about their families and the relationships they have seen or experienced. Higher-context students typically will not disclose what they consider personal information until they feel they are a part of the group. It is not uncommon for high-context students to do much more listening than speaking. The process of building relationships requires high levels of trust for these students and, in mixed-context groups, may seem to develop slowly.

One of the best ways to facilitate the participation of all students is through the use of open-ended questioning. These questions may be asked of the class as a whole, but care should be taken also to use strategies that give high-context students opportunities to be thoughtful, and to respond at their own pace.

## Communication and Conflict

The harmony of the group is an overarching consideration in high-context culture. In all communications, careful consideration of phrasing and intonation will take place before a comment is made. High-context students have internalized the tenet that their words must not have a negative impact on group connection. In a conflict, preserving harmony may well be favored over presenting facts. Relevant facts about the origins or ongoing interactions of a conflict may be omitted if they bring shame or a loss of respect to another group member, or if they threaten the continuation of the group. In low-context cultures, facts are given much more importance. It is assumed that by exploring the facts we can get to the truth, which helps us maintain healthy relationships, even if the connection is temporarily disrupted. Cultural differences in the handling of conflict create a high potential for disconnection between students of diverse cultural backgrounds.

Differences in communication styles between cultures can also inhibit connection. The rhythm and pattern of communication of high-context students can differ significantly from that of mainstream American students. For example, the time between speaker responses tends to be longer for high-context students.[15] If this pattern is misread, it might be assumed that the high-context student has nothing to contribute. While in mainstream American culture interrupting or leaping into a conversation is not seen as inappropriate behavior (especially if the individual has a pressing point to make), high-context students will rarely engage in this behavior.

## Gender Roles and Culture

Gender roles differ from culture to culture, and while some generalizations can be made (such as global inequalities in educational access, wages, and property rights), it is important to be aware that there are very different norms regarding behavior. Although a complete discussion of gender-role differences is impossible to present here, leaders should be mindful of some basic differences.

Many Asians value very different personality traits for males and females from Americans. For example, because of the strict hierarchical norms in Chinese and Japanese cultures, conformity, obedience, and kindness are valued in both men and women.[16] In much of Latin America and the Caribbean, the ideal woman is characterized as modest, weak, obedient to her husband, and dependent. Men, on the other hand, are expected to be independent, strong, willing to face danger, and dominant.[17] In a study of Mexican and American college students, researchers found that Mexican students of both genders valued family solidarity, while Americans of both genders valued independence and sexual egalitarianism.[18] There is ample evidence to suggest that traditional gender roles are in operation in much of Africa and the Middle East, as well. Students from these cultures (even second-generation immigrants) will exhibit differences from mainstream American students in their assumptions about behavior and values associated with gender.

## The Role of the Teacher/Leader in a Diverse Classroom

Teachers/ leaders have a responsibility to their students to determine their own personal level of comfort with issues of diversity. It's critically important for leaders to be aware of their own cultural identity and their experiences with inclusion and exclusion, and their personally held values, beliefs, and preferences. Creating a safe environment for diverse students requires a high level of comfort exploring the issues they confront. It also requires a high degree of self-knowledge, a willingness to learn from students, and an acceptance of values and attitudes that may differ from one's own.

African American and Hispanic students are, respectively, three and two times more likely to respond to teacher encouragement than to teacher demands.[19] For these students, a positive relationship with the teacher is a critical element in their performance. A positive relationship will also be an important element in freeing these students to explore gender roles, assumptions, and behaviors in mixed cultural groups.

High-context Asian students are likely to see the teacher as an authority figure requiring respect and deference. Particularly if they are recent immigrants, these students will not challenge or openly disagree with that authority. Allowing students to compare and contrast cultural gender roles, as well as to explore the positive and negative aspects of these norms without the interjection of the leader's opinions and values, will be necessary.

Many high-context Hispanic students mirror the roles, beliefs, and lifestyles of their parents.[20] Exploring attitudes and beliefs that differ from their parents' takes some getting used to for them: questioning family or community beliefs will be new behavior. Leaders can help by providing regular opportunities for students to use reflective journals. If students know their journals will be kept confidential—a critical requirement—there is a greater likelihood that they will express their feelings and ideas there first, as a way of testing them before revealing them to the class.

The leader of a diverse group of students engaging with this material must make sure that students do not totally embrace the cultural values of their mainstream peers without adequate reflection. Students can experience internal disruption and difficulty if they reject the values and norms of their originating culture without fully understanding and internalizing those they are using as replacements.[21] Providing additional resources (counseling, community organization support, or social workers) for these students may be necessary.

## FOUR OUTCOMES OF *MAKING CONNECTIONS*

**Growth-Fostering Relationships** Create mutually empowering, growth-fostering relationships within and across gender and culture.

**Positive Diversity** Create a process in which differences add positively to the experience. Together, boys and girls create something new and bring forth the greatest strengths within gender and across cultures.

**Mutual, Healthy Psychological Growth** Participate in each other's growth, move toward mutual psychological development, and participate in building the power, energy, and resilience of the "We."

**Emphasis on Full Human Potential** Develop less emphasis on gender or culture as dividing differences and more emphasis on the full human potential.

Adolescence is a time when differences are most prominent. *Making Connections* helps to institutionalize a vocabulary for understanding these differences, navigating relationships, facilitating individual growth, and building community. Through the process of the curriculum, differences are acknowledged and normalized to help to create a more inclusive "We."

# USING MAKING CONNECTIONS

## PROGRAM OBJECTIVES

The following program objectives are interrelated; each supports and strengthens the others. For example, as students become fluent in a new vocabulary, they begin to feel more empowered in their friendships. As they dispel stereotypes and begin to practice greater open-mindedness, they feel more connected in the classroom; this, in turn, results in an improved learning atmosphere. Some outcomes will be observed right away. Others may evolve over time, particularly as students revisit and practice the concepts learned during formal program sessions.

1. **An enhanced learning environment.** As students learn to engage across their differences, the class becomes more connected, more inclusive, and the learning environment improves for everyone, teacher included.
2. **The creation of a class "We" or a school or community "We."** This can be described as a "connected classroom" or a stronger *experience* of community and a more connected school.
3. **Building "conscious coeducation."** This describes an educational context in which empathetic understanding of gender and cultural differences works to expand possibilities for healthy connections in the classroom and facilitates cross-gender and cross-cultural friendships and friendship groups.
4. **A valuable vocabulary.** Students become fluent in a new language that they intuitively understand and quickly begin to use to describe and improve relational dynamics. This language often becomes part of the overall school culture. Students shift from blaming ("*You* are the problem") to mutual responsibility ("*We*'re having a disconnect"). The language resonates with, and affirms, their desire for positive connections.
5. **Breaking down gender and cultural stereotypes.** Through the dialogue process, the hidden curriculum of gender is brought out into the open. Students learn how to engage respectfully around differences in opinion, experience, and outlook that formerly provoked tension and disconnection. This results in stronger connections and increased understanding.
6. **Tools to address, understand, and appreciate differences of all kinds.** The dialogue process, a specific method of inquiry, can be applied to address not only gender differences, but other differences such as race, ethnicity, socioeconomic class, learning ablitlies, sexual orientation, and religion.

7. **Empowerment in friendships.** Students grow in their capacity to deal with conflicts and disconnects. They can more readily identify relational impasses and problems, and can apply their new awareness and language to move through conflict and disconnection toward reconnection. Friendships across gender and culture can grow and develop.
8. **A more connected, "peaceable" school.** This program offers individual students an antidote to disconnection and violence. It also provides a model for solving community problems together and encourages the bystander to be a caring witness in a connected community.
9. **A solid foundation on which to build other learning.** This curriculum can serve as a natural springboard into a variety of other topics for which curricula already exist— bullying and violence prevention, conflict resolution, social justice, literature, social studies, and other content areas.
10. **A basis for thinking about cultural messages.** This curriculum addresses ways in which the media reinforces, impacts, and defines "cool" and healthy relationships.

## PEDAGOGY OF SESSIONS

The essence of the curriculum is built on an interweaving of the conceptual and experiential learning processes. This process begins at the verbal and conceptual level and is reinforced through kinesthetic learning, ultimately leading to and reinforcing the student's ability to apply and transfer the skills and concepts learned. These processes are interrelated; each builds on and spirals with the others. All seven core sessions are constructed within this framework. Components of this process are described below.

**Conceptual/Verbal Learning**–Students are provided with theory and language to describe their experience of connection, disconnection, reconnection and the "We."

**Experiential Learning**–Students access their own past and present experiences.

**Kinesthetic Learning**–Students engage directly through physical involvement and witnessing others.

**Observing**–Students witness the group and observe each other as they participate in interactive activities.

**Reflecting**–Students bring their observations and experience to consciousness through journal writing and class discussions.

**Active Listening**–Students learn about boys' and girls' friendships and each other's answers to the "dialogue" questions by listening to each other.

**Sharing**–Students share their thoughts, feelings, and individual ways of connecting, disconnecting, and reconnecting in same- and cross-gender small groups,

**Dialoging** – Students share, ask, and discuss questions and answers in a structured, mixed-gender, whole class dialogue.

**Applying and Transferring** – Students apply their new knowledge and skills regarding connection, disconnection, reconnection, and the "We" to their lives at school and home.

# WHO SHOULD PARTICIPATE?

*Making Connections* is appropriate to use with middle-school and high-school students. Students will participate at the level of their experience, understanding, and developmental stage. Because of this, the curriculum can be repeated and applied throughout middle and high school. This helps students become more aware of their growth and development.

## Middle School

Middle school might aptly be described as a rapidly changing culture of connections, disconnections, and reconnections. During early adolescence, girls and boys undergo enormous physical, psychological, and cognitive changes that reverberate through their relationships. If one follows the lives of middle-school students throughout a typical school day, the disconnects between boys, between girls, and between boys and girls are constant and repetitive, yet are rarely processed or addressed. As one seventh-grade girl commented, "I never knew you could *talk* about relationships; I thought they just happened."

The middle-school environment itself can contribute to students' sense of fragmentation. Many girls and boys find themselves in a new and larger school, where they move for the first time from class to class, subject to subject, with different peer groupings in each class. As a result, many students feel more isolated and less like a coherent part of a community, and therefore less part of a "We."

Students are marginalized in many ways by race, ethnicity, class, sexual identity, learning abilities, physical appearance, and deviation from gender norms—as in not being a "real" boy or a "girly" girl. There is a strict code of fitting in, with the dominant voice of each gender group reinforced by TV, film, music, popular magazines, and older students. For those boys who are not "macho" or athletic, or girls who are not "cool" or "hot," there is, at best, the alternative of fitting into some more marginalized group, or, at worst, the experience of personal shaming and isolation. The upsurge of school violence has often been traced to the shaming and ostracism in boy culture, with a more and more isolated boy turning into a loner with a grudge and possibly a gun. Other boys or girls may turn to drugs or alcohol, become depressed or suicidal, or develop eating disorders.[22]

In a classroom and school that values authentic connection—and develops a class "We" and a school "We"—more marginalized voices have greater opportunity to speak and be heard, and even to shine. They are brought into the mainstream not by becoming part of the dominant culture, but through the dialogue between different voices. The more the marginalized person who may not fit in develops a voice that can be heard, the more the conversation deepens, and the healthier the school and classroom become. The inclusion/exclusion dance that occurs in middle school keeps students from connecting with each other; they fear being left out and rejected by particular groups. The dialogue process encourages connections across groups, drawing attention to the divisions that exist in the school and helping to bridge these disconnections.

## High School

In high school, social and psychological isolation, the result of profound disconnection, appears to be a risk factor for violence, alcohol and drug abuse, depression, and suicide. These are the clinical manifestations of the more normal difficulties of adolescents. High-school students encounter the same relationship challenges as do preteens, with the added issues of negotiating dating and sexuality and use of alcohol and drugs. Optional Sessions A, B, and C may be especially relevant for high-school students.

Examples of healthy relationships are rare in the media, and with a large number of marriages ending in divorce, perhaps rare in their family settings as well. In a media-driven culture that provides few examples of relationships based on mutuality and respect, the combination of sexual attraction and poorly developed relational skills can be very destructive. In gender dialogues with hundreds of high-school students, the authors have heard talk about how, all too often, male/female relationships are based on dominance, sometimes with physical and verbal abuse. In addition, the new sexual behaviors of "friendships with benefits," or "hooking up" clearly reflect relational disconnection.[23] Yet the authors have also heard how strongly teenagers are yearning to be in safe relationships both within their own gender group and across gender. They yearn for this refuge and will work hard to create it when given the opportunity. As one eleventh grader said, "I've been waiting ten years to be able to ask these questions." Another added, "This is the *best* thing we have ever done at school."

Teens are ripe for this work, and take to it enthusiastically. The dialogue process engages students and encourages honesty, reflection, laughter, and heartfelt discussion. In high school, students begin to have more experiences and contact with others across differences of race, ethnicity, and socioeconomics. They are able to begin working with these experiences using language and concepts that allow for more subtlety, depth, and authentic engagement.

## THE ROLE OF THE TEACHER/LEADER

A skilled educator can lead the program sessions: for example, a male or female teacher, counselor, coach, or school administrator. In some instances, a male/female team of co-leaders may prove most beneficial.

The activities in the *Making Connections* curriculum work to establish a safe climate. This safe and respectful atmosphere becomes the foundation that supports both the individual's and the group's process in establishing a climate of trust in which different views are accepted and welcomed. Individuals and the group as a whole are empowered to take risks and to engage in a respectful dialogue around differences—whether they are racial, ethnic, socioeconomic, or physical. The teacher/counselor/leader becomes a model for students by acknowledging and naming differences, allowing students to feel safe and engage in dialogue that addresses differences and allows nondominant voices to speak and be heard. Reading through the sessions and the guidelines for facilitating dialogue (p 68) before beginning will familiarize teachers/leaders with the material and vocabulary and prepare them for guiding successful dialogues.

If teachers feel uncomfortable raising a particular issue, it is important to acknowledge this, demonstrating that teachers don't always know the "correct" language to use. By taking time, trusting the process, and being willing to take the risks of being in new, evolving territory, teachers model a process that allows for discovering new pathways that lead to authentic connection. Teachers need to be willing to "hold" and stay with an uncomfortable moment in order to clarify what students are trying to communicate. These moments can impact an entire group, and give everyone permission to get to what is essential for the movement of the group.

## WHEN AND WHERE TO IMPLEMENT THE SESSIONS

Program sessions can be implemented in a range of school settings, from primary subject areas to extracurricular activities to weekend retreats for specific student groups. Although sessions can begin at any time of year, many teachers use *Making Connections* at the start of the year to build a sense of inclusion and connection among students. Others use the program to help consolidate the class as the year progresses.

Whenever possible, it is important to link program topics to existing subject matter and relevant areas of study. For example:

- In English classes, character and plot development in literature can be viewed through the lens of connection/disconnection
- In Social Studies and History classes, discussions of community-building,

human rights, political systems, democracy, etc., can be enhanced by an understanding of the dynamics of connection/disconnection and of the benefits of dialogue

- In Health classes, program sessions can support the development of students' social and emotional well-being
- In guidance and counseling groups, dialogue tools can be used to resolve conflicts and support the development of healthy relationships
- In homeroom or advisory program sessions can promote team-building
- Before or during team-building events, leadership classes, or mentoring programs, sessions can be used to foster cooperation and understanding among students
- For training student leaders, peer mentors, or peer counselors, the program addresses essential issues

## SESSION FORMAT

The core of *Making Connections* consists of seven forty-five to sixty minute sessions. All sessions are essential to the program's success and should be taught sequentially, as presented in this guide. Sessions can be taught on consecutive days, every other day, or two times per week, as your schedule allows. To maintain momentum, schedule program sessions *at least* once a week. The ideal group size is twelve to twenty-five students.

Three additional optional sessions are included that address major issues that influence gender relationships, including the impact of media on gender stereotypes, qualities of healthy and unhealthy dating relationships, and the impact of drugs and alcohol on relationships. These sessions can be added at the discretion of the teacher/leader, depending on the age and level of experience of the class or group.

Each session includes the following:

**Learning Objectives**: Objectives identify what students will be able to demonstrate at the end of the unit and help teachers/leaders align each session to state standards. The importance of this work is recognized in the standards-based educational philosophy of many schools throughout the country. State and federal frameworks were considered for all sessions.

**Agenda**: A brief outline of what students will do during the session. Writing the agenda on the board or on chart paper allows students to know what to expect from each session.

**Materials**: A list of all the materials needed for the session. All handouts are located at the end of the session and are reproducible. Handouts can also be printed out from the CD included.

**Supporting Activities**: The supporting activities listed can be found in Appendix I and reinforce basic concepts introduced in the session.

**Introduction**: A suggested format for introducing the session.

**Activities**: Three to five activities that foster experiential learning through the following formats: Brainstorms, Writing, Role-Plays, Sharing, Observations, Reflections, Generating Dialogue.

**Teaching Tips**: Tips include additional information, explanations, and reflections.

**Cultural Considerations**: Provides ways to adapt activities and/or concepts for culturally diverse groups.

## REINFORCING *MAKING CONNECTIONS*: TRANSFERRING SKILLS AND CONCEPTS

- Continue to use the vocabulary of connection, disconnection, reconnection, and the "*We*."
- Invite students to work together to address problems that arise in class. For example: "We have a problem. People aren't listening to each other. What are some things we can do to solve this problem?"
- Take advantage of class beginnings and endings to build a sense of connection among students. For instance, start by setting goals for individuals *and* for the class. End by asking students to name any constructive actions they observed that contributed to the "*We*."
- Reframe bullying, exclusion, and gender-shaming among students as disconnections that hurt individuals as well as damage the class "*We*."
- View relational disconnections in the classroom as "teachable moments." Encourage students to draw upon language and concepts learned in program sessions, while you help students "hold the *We*" through these disconnects.
- Offer students frequent opportunities to work in small same-gender and mixed-gender groups.
- Call for "dialogue" on an ongoing basis. Revisit insights from the gender dialogue. Address new issues that impact the class "*We*." Use the dialogue technique to explore topics in literature or history through the lens of connection, disconnection, and reconnection.
- Reward students for sharing and participating in ways that contribute to the "*We*."

# BUILDING A SCHOOL COMMUNITY AND CULTURE THAT SUPPORTS *MAKING CONNECTIONS*

Ways to promote the core values of the curriculum throughout the school:

- Introduce concepts from the curriculum to teachers during staff development meetings and to parents during parent association meetings.
- Create a common vocabulary and core values based on the curriculum for the entire community, including school staff, parents, and students, to share.
- Model respectful relationships within the school community.
- Develop ways to address disconnections among members of the school community.
- Have clear and consistent consequences for bullying or sexually harassing behavior.
- Create a safe space for students to get counseling about relationship problems.

# THE LANGUAGE OF CONNECTION

*"I never knew you could talk about relationships. I thought they just happened!"*[1]

## Introduction

Welcome everyone to the group, give an overview of the program, and answer any preliminary questions participants may have. Include the following points:

> *The goal of this work is to learn about the importance of building strong connections in our personal lives and in school and how to make these connections with others. We'll be talking about the strengths and weaknesses of same-gender relationships: girls' friendships with other girls and boys' friendships with other boys. We'll be working toward a "gender dialogue" in which you will have the chance to ask each other honest and important questions about your lives as girls and young women and your lives as boys and young men. We'll talk about gender and cultural differences and commonalities, with the goal of better understanding each other and building a stronger community together.*

## Brainstorm: Defining Terms

Note: *Before doing this activity with students, please review the definition of terms on* **Handout 1: Definitions** *and become familiar with them. If you chose to distribute this handout to students, do not do so until the end of the activity.*

Distribute **Handout 2: Qualities of Connection Chart**.

Write the following four words across the top of the board:

> *Connection, Disconnection, Reconnection, the Class "We."*

Quickly brainstorm lists of words associated with each term, drawing upon the following examples. Record answers on the board underneath each term. Have students list answers on the handout.

**Learning Objectives**

Students will:

- Learn a conceptual framework for understanding relationships
- Be able to discuss connection/disconnection/reconnection in relation to their own experience
- Understand connection, disconnection, reconnection and the class "We"

**Agenda**

- Introduction
- Brainstorm: Defining Terms
- Role-Play: Silent Movies or Writing: Literature Connections
- Writing: Record a Personal Experience
- Homework: Observations

**Materials**

- Handout 1: Definitions (p 31)
- Handout 2: Qualities of Connection Chart (p 32)
- Handout 3: Silent Movie Squares (p 33)
- Handout 4: Literature Excerpts (p 34)
- Handout 5: Observations (p 36)

[1]This and other quotations at the start of each session are from participants in *Making Connections*.

Supporting Activities

These activities reinforce basic concepts introduced in this session:

- Diagramming the "We" (p 89)
- Class Mission (p 90)
- Class Quilt (p 90)

## Cultural Consideration

For recent immigrants (Asian, African, Caribbean, and Eastern European) and Native American students, brainstorming may initially be an uncomfortable exercise, especially if English is not their first language. The idea of expressing the first thing that comes to mind, without thinking of how it will affect the group or their relationship with the group, is not common to these cultures. Engaging in brainstorming activities may also be difficult if they have experienced exclusion as minority populations within the school setting.

In these cases, provide the whole class with a chance to answer individually and give them a few moments to self-reflect and write in their journals. This allows those students who need it a chance to be thoughtful about their response.

**Connection**: *What do we mean when we say* connection? *Think of a connection in your life right now. This could be with a friend, a relative, a teacher, a neighbor, or someone from a team or club. What words, pictures, or feelings come to mind when you think about your connection with this person or these people?*

**Disconnection**: *Have any of you ever felt disconnected from someone? What do we mean by disconnection? What is a "disconnect"?*

**Reconnection**: *Can anyone define* reconnection? *When you think of reconnection, what other words/feelings/pictures come to mind?*

**The Class "We"**: *What does a classroom look like and feel like when there is a sense of inclusion and a spirit of working well together? What would you imagine is meant by the Class "We"? If the context is not a classroom, use Team "We," Group "We," etc.*

Examples of student answers:

| Connection | Disconnection | Reconnection | "We" |
|---|---|---|---|
| friendship | problems | apology | peace |
| honesty | lying | forgiveness | equality |
| encouragement | distrust | hug | community |
| smiles | tears | reacceptance | patience |
| trust | teasing | together again | circle |

Refer to **Handout 1: Definitions** to supplement or clarify student definitions and descriptions. It can also be passed out to students as a reference after they have completed the brainstorm.

## Role-Play: Silent Movies

Cut out the squares on **Handout 3: Silent Movie Squares**.

Divide students into single- or mixed-gender groups of three or four.

Give each group one Silent Movie Square from Handout 3 that contains one relational term: *connection*, *disconnection*, *reconnection* or the "*We*." Make sure all four terms are used.

Directions:

*Here's the challenge: come up with a way to express the meaning of your word to the rest of the class – through movement. The class will try to guess your word, based on the way your bodies are arranged, your postures, symbolic gestures, or movements. Although physical fighting reflects a disconnection, think of other types of disconnection.*

Guidelines:

- Everyone in the group participates.
- No talking in the final presentation.
- Communicate only through movement.

Allow groups seven to ten minutes to prepare in different areas of the room and/or hallway.

One at a time, have each group enact their word. After each presentation, audience observers decide whether the role-play is about *connection*, *disconnection*, *reconnection*, or the "We." Ask students to notice how each role-play makes them feel.

Ask students to describe each quality, based on what they see in each silent movie. Have students write their responses in the chart in **Handout 2: Qualities of Connection**. Simultaneously, add student responses to the original lists on the board.

## Alternative Activity: Literature Connections

This activity can be done in lieu of Silent Movies.

Distribute **Handout 4: Literature Excerpts**.

Read one literature excerpt at a time with the class. Ask students to take note of connections/disconnections between the characters as they listen to the reading. Discuss the qualities of connection and disconnection and direct students to add responses to **Handout 2: Qualities of Connection**.

> **TEACHING TIP**
>
> Everyone is responsible for creating the sense of "We" in the classroom, including the leader/teacher. Explore with students the role of the leader in setting the tone for connection or disconnection and helping to create the sense of "We."

The first excerpt illustrates the transformation of a disconnection into a connection between a teacher and student. It can be used as a springboard for a discussion on connection/disconnection/reconnection.

The second excerpt illustrates the power of Tom Sawyer's connection with his aunt and an attempted, but failed, connection with Becky Thatcher. It shows the risk involved in connection between boys and girls and underscores the premise that it takes more than one willing participant to achieve connection.

Ask students to find further examples of connection/disconnection from their own literature class or personal reading, paying particular attention to the relationships as they read.

## Writing: Record a Personal Experience

Ask students to record a personal experience in relationships. Afterward, say the following:

### reflection

If a student laughs at another's experience, use this as an opportunity to point out the "disconnect" within the group. "How does the 'We' feel right now in this room? Connected? Disconnected? Solid? Shaky?... " Emphasize that respectful, attentive listening makes it possible for others to take risks and to be more honest.

*We've done a great job defining these concepts. Each one of you also has wisdom about these terms based on personal experience.*

*Take a minute now to think about your own relationships. Describe one personal experience you have had of either connection, disconnection, or reconnection with someone else or within a group.*

*Take a few minutes to write about this experience. What happened? How did it make you feel? What did you learn from the experience?*

Ask for two or three student volunteers to read or describe their experiences to the class.

The teacher/leader may choose to share a personal experience of connection, disconnection, or reconnection with the class.

### cultural consideration

Students who believe they have been excluded from membership in other school groups (formal or informal) because of their diversity characteristics may raise that exclusion during this activity or during the first few sessions of the group. How these concerns, experiences, or feelings are addressed by the class, and, most importantly, whether these students feel supported by the teacher/leader, will often determine the level of their ongoing participation in the group. If students raise the issue of their culture, ethnicity, sexual orientation, or other diversity characteristics, ensure that they have the time, attention, and support of the class community while expressing their thoughts or feelings.

Ask students: *What could have happened differently to make that experience a positive one for you?* or, *What can we, as a community, do to make sure that doesn't happen in our community?*

## Homework: Observations

Distribute **Handout 5: Observations**.

Review the assignment and answer any outstanding questions. Emphasize the importance of not using people's names in this exercise. Tell students that they will share their observations at the start of the next class.

Session 1, Handout 1 Date ____________________

Name ________________________________________________________________

# DEFINITIONS

**Connection**: Connection describes an experience of contact, joining, or interacting with another person or among a group of people that benefits or fosters the growth of the people involved. Connection can be felt in varying degrees; in other words, you can feel more or less connected to someone else. For instance, you may feel simply happy to be with someone after a period of being apart. Or you may feel a sense of belonging and acceptance working together with a team or group of people. Or you may feel a deep bond with a close friend after a meaningful conversation. We tend to notice connection when there's a change—an increase or decrease—in our sense of connectedness with others. (See page 4 for a detailed list of the qualities of growth-fostering connection.)

**Disconnection:** Disconnection is a separation or a break in a relationship with another person or among a group of people. Like connection, disconnection can take a number of forms and is usually felt in varying degrees—from minor disappointment to significant devastation. For example, you may not have spoken to a friend in several days and you may miss that feeling of connection. Or you might feel excluded from a group game or activity, or you might witness another student's being shamed or teased and you don't know what to do. Or perhaps you feel utterly misunderstood by a friend. Disconnects often generate feelings of hurt or anger. Not speaking up due to fear is a further disconnect. There is often a concurrent breakdown of respect, inclusion, honesty, and engagement. Disconnection of groups of people can be direct, as in racial discrimination, or indirect, in the form of ignoring, excluding, or not creating a safe space for the expression of differences. Cultural differences may foster disconnections, especially when they are unseen, unacknowledged, or marginalized.

**Reconnection**: In reconnection, both (or all) people in the relationship move back from a sense or experience of separateness into joining. This process can sometimes result in a new and expanded connection that benefits from what has been learned from the disconnections.

**The "We":** The "We" describes the experience of belonging for all members of a given community. In a school setting, the class "We" or group "We" describes the experience of a "connected classroom" in which each student feels respected and knows that he or she can make a difference, individually and/or collectively. In such a class, there is room for every student to make mistakes, to try new things, to be creative, to ask for help, to reach out to another, to be himself or herself and speak the truth of her/his experience. This is not always comfortable or easy. Here are some examples of the class "We" or group "We" in action: students listen to and validate each other's ideas; students recognize and respect each other's differences; a disagreement gets resolved respectfully; a student voices her/his minority opinion in safety. The classroom "We" contributes to the all-school "We," or to any connected community.

Session 1, Handout 2

Date ______________________

Name ________________________________________________________________

# QUALITIES OF CONNECTION CHART

Directions: Fill out the chart below with your observations.

| Connection | Disconnection | Reconnection | The "We" |
|---|---|---|---|
| | | | |

Session 1, Handout 3

Date ______________

Name ______________________________

# SILENT MOVIE SQUARES

For this activity, students work in groups of three or four. Cut out enough squares so that each group gets one square and each relational term is used.

| | |
|---|---|
| **Connection** | **Connection** |
| **Disconnection** | **Disconnection** |
| **Reconnection** | **Reconnection** |
| **The "We"** | **The "We"** |

Date ____________________

Name ________________________________________________________________

# LITERATURE EXCERPTS

**Excerpt 1**

Mr. Lema, the sixth-grade teacher, greeted me and assigned me a desk. He then introduced me to the class. I was so nervous and scared at that moment when everyone's eyes were on me that I wished I were with Papa and Roberto picking cotton.

After taking roll, Mr. Lema gave the class the assignment for the first hour. "The first thing we have to do this morning is finish reading the story we began yesterday," he said enthusiastically. He walked up to me, handed me an English book, and asked me to read. "We are on page 125," he said politely.

When I heard this, I felt my blood rush to my head; I felt dizzy.

"Would you like to read?" he asked hesitantly. I opened the book to page 125. My mouth was dry. My eyes began to water. I could not begin. "You can read later," Mr. Lema said understandingly.

For the rest of the reading period I kept getting angrier and angrier with myself. I should have read, I thought to myself.

During recess, I went to the restroom and opened my English book to page 125. I began to read in a low voice, pretending I was in class. There were many words I did not know. I closed the book and headed back to the classroom.

Mr. Lema was sitting at his desk correcting papers. When I entered he looked up at me and smiled. I felt better. I walked up to him and asked if he could help me with the new words.

"Gladly," he said.

**Excerpt 2**

There was something about Aunt Polly's manner when she kissed Tom that swept away his low spirits and made him light-hearted and happy again. He started to school, and had the luck of coming upon Becky Thatcher at the head of Meadow Lane. His mood always determined his manner. Without a moment's hesitation he ran to her and said:

"I acted mighty mean today, Becky, and I'm so sorry. I won't ever, ever do it that way again as long as ever I live... please make up, won't you?"

The girl stopped and looked him scornfully in the face. "I'll thank you to keep yourself to yourself, Mr. Thomas Sawyer. I'll never speak to you again." She tossed her head and passed on.

Tom was so stunned that he had not even presence of mind to say, "Who cares, Miss Smarty?" until the right time to say it had gone by. So he said nothing. But he was in a fine rage, nevertheless. He moped into the school-yard wishing she were a boy, and imagining how he would trounce her if she were.

He presently encountered her and delivered a stinging remark as he passed. She hurled one in return, and the angry breach was complete...

Excerpted from *The Adventures of Tom Sawyer,* by Mark Twain.

Session 1, Handout 5 Date ____________________

Name ____________________________________________

# OBSERVATIONS

**Be a Conscious Observer**

Relationships are happening all around you: connections, disconnections, and reconnections between students (and adults, too) in the cafeteria, the library, the gym, during classes, on playing fields, up and down hallways—every minute and everywhere in school.

Your assignment: observe and describe in writing at least one "connect" and one "disconnect" that don't directly involve you. Listen to conversations, track tones of voices, watch body language, sense emotions.

Use the 3 Rs

- Record your observations as soon as you can.
- Remember not to mention individual names.
- Reflect and notice how the interactions make you feel. Record these feelings, too.

**Connection:**

**Disconnection:**

# RELATIONAL MOVEMENT

*"Disconnection happens as much as connection. You can learn from it and have a tighter relationship afterwards."*

## Introduction

*Relationships are always in movement. They move back and forth between connection and disconnection. Sometimes connection can grow into even stronger connection, or disconnection can spiral into even more disconnection. After a disconnect, it sometimes takes time for a relationship to move toward reconnection. Relationships can be seen as dances we create with each other as expressed in the movement of connection, diconnection, reconnection and the "We." Think about your own friendships. Do they stay the same, or do they change?*

**Learning Objectives**

Students will:

- Understand that relationships are dynamic, always moving and changing
- Understand and demonstrate that connection and disconnection are not static states of being or feeling
- Describe the ways movement toward connection promotes growth and well-being
- Discuss the ways attitudes and actions influence the quality of our connection with others

## Sharing: Observations about Connection

Before beginning this activity, review Active Listening skills on page 91.

Distribute **Handout 1: Movement of Connection** and **Handout 2: Movement of Disconnection.**

Ask students to work in pairs and share one homework observation of either connection or disconnection. Each student should ask his or her partner the following three questions and record answers on the appropriate handout. Remind students not to use the names of people when answering.

1. What did you *see*? What did the connection/disconnection *look* like?
2. What did you *feel*? What did the connection/disconnection *feel* like to you? What might people have been feeling?
3. What might this situation *lead* to? What might happen *next* in this relationship?

### Cultural Consideration

Strategy Tip: To children from cultures that deeply value community, in which the individual's sense of self is derived from his or her place in the community or family, the list of disconnecting behaviors may seem to be extreme. Some students might even feel that they would never do anything like interrupt, disrupt the task, or criticize.

Agenda

- Introduction
- Sharing: Observations about Connection
- Role-Play: Connections or Disconnections
- Homework: Your Choice

Materials

- Handout 1: Movement of Connection (p 40)
- Handout 2: Movement of Disconnection (p 41)
- Handout 3: Role-Play Squares (p 42)
- Handout 4: Your Choice: Moving Toward or Moving Away? (p 43)

Supporting Activities

These activities reinforce basic concepts introduced in this session:

- Practices for Active Listening (p 91)
- How are *We*? (p 91)
- Community Survey (p 92)

Ask for volunteers to share one observation with the entire class and answer each of the three questions. Record on the board. Have students record their observations on their handouts.

Sample answers:

CONNECTION

| Looks Like | Feels Like | Might Lead To |
|---|---|---|
| Two students working out details of an after-school activity | Inclusive, caring, sharing | Friendship |

DISCONNECTION

| Looks Like | Feels Like | Might Lead To |
|---|---|---|
| Name-calling in the hall distrust, shame | Rejection, hurt | A fight |

## Role-Play: Connection and Disconnection

Divide students into small groups of two, three, or four. Groups can be either same or mixed gender.

Cut out squares from **Handout 3: Role-Play Squares** and distribute one to each group. Be sure that all themes are used.

Have each group write an original script dramatizing their theme. The role-play should be realistic, based on actual experience or observation. Explain:

*Use what you know best: either a personal experience of one of the group members; something you've observed at school; or a typical situation for students your age. Although physical fighting reflects a disconnection, this is not an appropriate example for this exercise.*

Explain the guidelines:

1. Communicate your theme through both dialogue and body language.
2. The role-play should last as long as it takes to get your theme across.
3. Each group member needs to write out the full script in order to participate.

Allow groups approximately 15 minutes to write and rehearse their scripts.

CULTURAL CONSIDERATION

Processing Tip: If your classroom is a diverse mix of cultures, have students add to or develop their own list of connecting and disconnecting behaviors before assigning this activity. Then let them have small-group discussions about the items they have in common as well as the differences they see. Be aware of cultural differences in connecting and disconnecting behaviors as they develop their role-play script.

Have each group perform their role-play for the class. After each role-play, ask the other groups to take thirty seconds to come to a consensus on two questions:

1. What is the *theme* of the role-play? See if the class agrees.
2. Do you think *relational movement* is possible at this point in the scenario? Can the relationship move? Or does it need more time?

Refer to **Handout 1: Movement of Connection** and **Handout 2: Movement of Disconnection**, and fill in the chart, this time using information from each role-play scenario.

## Homework: Your Choice — Moving Toward or Moving Away?

Distribute and review **Handout 4: Your Choice—Moving Toward or Moving Away?** Ask for a volunteer to read aloud the directions. Let students know that they will be asked to share responses in the next session.

Session 2, Handout 1

Date ______________________

Name ____________________________________________________________

# MOVEMENT OF CONNECTION

| What do you see?<br>Looks Like | What do you feel?<br>Feels Like | What might happen?<br>Might Lead to |
| --- | --- | --- |
| | | |

Session 2, Handout 2

Date ______________

Name ______________________________________________

# MOVEMENT OF DISCONNECTION

| What do you see?<br>Looks Like | What do you feel?<br>Feels Like | What might happen?<br>Might Lead to |
|---|---|---|
| | | |

Date ____________________

Name ____________________________________________

# role-play squares

For this activity, students work in groups of two, three, or four. Cut out enough strips so that each group gets one strip and each theme is used.

| Connection |
|---|
| Connection → Disconnection → Reconnection |
| Disconnection → Connection |
| Disconnection |
| Connection |
| Connection → Disconnection |
| Disconnection → Reconnection |
| Disconnection |

Session 2, Handout 4

Date ____________________

Name ______________________________________________

# YOUR CHOICE: MOVING TOWARD OR MOVING AWAY?

**Does this response/attitude/action lead me toward or away from connection?**

- We often have more power than we realize to influence which way a relationship moves: toward or away from connection. The words we choose to say, the attitude we choose to adopt, and the actions we choose to take can move us closer to or farther away from connection with another person or group.
- Sometimes, especially when we're upset, we forget that we have a choice and simply react on the basis of our emotions. But even then, we can step back afterward and make a mindful choice about what to say or do next.

**ASSIGNMENT**

Pay attention to your relationships this week. Notice how often you have choices about how to respond to a person or situation. Write about and/or illustrate an instance where you did or did not consciously choose what to say or do next—and about the results of your choice. In which direction did the relationship move: toward or away from connection?

**1. Describe how the relationship moved in this direction.**

**2. If I responded impulsively and reactively it looked like...**

**3. If I reflected and chose consciously how to react, it might have looked like...**

# SAME-GENDER CONNECTS AND DISCONNECTS

*"Our friendships are really important to us."*

## Introduction

*Today we're going to look at same-gender relationships: at the connections and disconnections between girls and the connections and disconnections between boys. What's similar about girls' and boys' friendships? Do you think there's anything different about the ways boys and girls connect—and disconnect? What can girls' and boys' friendships teach us about girls, about boys, about ourselves, and about being a friend?*

## Brainstorm: Same-Gender Friendships

Divide the class into same-gender groups of approximately three students each.

Distribute **Handout 1a: Girl Friendships** and **Handout 1b: Boy Friendships**

Review handouts with the class. Point out that group members may have different answers and opinions. This is to be expected, since every person's experience is unique. Remind students that everyone's opinion should be noted and respected.

Ask groups to select one person to record and report the group's responses.

Allow groups 15 minutes or so to list answers in depth, based on their own experience with friendships. Invite groups to move into separate spaces, where they will be able to talk privately.

Move from group to group, checking on progress and assisting students as needed. If some groups finish early, encourage students to dig a little deeper. Ask: *What about relationships in the classroom? Are there differences between groups of girls/boys? Are there cultural differences?*

**Learning Objectives**

Students will:

- Describe the connections and disconnections that occur in same-gender relationships
- Discuss what is similar and different about friendships between boys and friendships between girls
- Deepen awareness of how gender stereotypes influence perception

**Agenda**

- Introduction
- Brainstorm: Same-Gender Friendships
- Sharing: Class Discussion
- Writing: Letter of Appreciation

**Materials**

- Handout 1a: Girl Friendships (p 49)
- Handout 1b: Boy Friendships (p 50)
- Handout 2: Letter of Appreciation (p 51)
- Paper and envelopes for letters

**Supporting Activity**

This activity reinforces the concepts of this session.

- Stereotypes (p 92)

*Suggestion*: If staff is available, it can be helpful for a male teacher to meet with the boys and a female teacher to meet with the girls.

## Sharing: Class Discussion

### avoid stereotypes

Help students avoid stereotyping either "boys" or "girls" as a group; generalizations can be easily modified by the use of the word "some." For instance, reframe the blanket statement "Guys are really selfish" as "*Some* guys are really selfish." "All girls like to gossip" becomes "Some girls like to gossip."

Bring the full class together. Create a chart on the board (see sample).

Ask each reporter to read aloud small-group responses to question 1. Have all reporters of one gender group go first, followed by reporters of the other gender. Continue with the next two questions. Reinforce active listening skills.

Have two volunteers, one girl and one boy, record answers on the board. Indicate answers from more than one student with a check.

Sample chart with student answers:

**Same-Gender Connections: Strengths**

| GIRLS | BOYS |
|---|---|
| talk on the phone | show loyalty ✓ |
| just listen | understand if you beat on them |
| give advice | don't have much to say |
| sympathize with you | play rough |
| feel close | like sports ✓ |
| trust | understand each other |
| can read your feelings | come together when playing sports |

**Same-Gender Disconnections: Difficulties**

| GIRLS | BOYS |
|---|---|
| Fight over boys | Some guys are really selfish |
| Have issues over degrees of popularity ✓ | Getting left out of a new friendship |
| Spread rumors | Pressure to be cool |
| Hold a grudge | Play fighting can get out of hand |
| Popular girls ignore girls who are different (spoken by a group of hearing-impaired girls) | Tease boys who are different and not good at sports |
| Talk behind each other's backs ✓ | Don't always talk about feelings |
| Racial divisions among girls | Racial divisions among boys |
| Girls mature at different levels | Play "cool" to impress girls |
| Can be very emotionally reactive over small things | Taunt each other |

When all groups have reported their responses, ask the class the following reflection questions:

1. *Is there anything that surprises you or that stands out about what the other gender reported?*

2. *Is there anything different about the ways girls and boys connect in their relationships? What do you think is most different?*

3. *What do boys' friendships and girls' friendships have in common?*

4. *How about disconnection? Are there similarities between boys' and girls' disconnections? Are there any differences?*

5. *Are there any differences within gender groups among boys or among girls that have not yet been acknowledged? Example: In one group with a significant number of hearing-impaired girls, relationships between hearing and hearing-impaired girls became an important focus of discussion. "Because we can't communicate with words in the same way, other kids don't see us and we feel like we are invisible." In another group, a few boys said, "Some of us really don't care about sports and we feel put down and not valued for who we are."*

### Cultural Consideration

Issues may arise with "gay" or "lesbian" labels, stereotypes, or slurs used to put down and sexualize close same-gender relationships. Leaders must pay close attention to the group dynamics, ensuring that students are not excluded or wounded during this exploration. Immediately confront disconnecting behavior. If this behavior continues, have students discuss the use of disconnecting words and behaviors and their effects on individual students and on the class as a whole.

## Writing: Letter of Appreciation

Set up the assignment with a thirty-second visualization:

> *Everyone take a moment to close your eyes and call to mind a person in your life—someone the same gender as you—who really matters to you. Scan through your relationships and choose one person. This could be a friend, a family member, a neighbor, a teacher, a coach, or someone else who matters to you. You will write a letter to this person expressing your appreciation. It is your choice to send it or not.*

Distribute **Handout 2: Letter of Appreciation**. Also hand out a sheet of lined paper to each student. Review the assignment together.

Offer a few starter questions such as: *Can you think of a special time or a fun time you spent together? What do you appreciate about this person? What has this person said or done that's meant a lot to you? How has your relationship with this person helped you to grow?*

If anyone is confused, suggest a line to get started (Dear ___, I've been thinking about you).

If time allows, ask for volunteers to share the qualities of the person they chose that they appreciate and respect.

*Note*: If there is not enough time to complete this activity, it can be assigned as homework.

Session 3, Handout 1a

Date ____________________

Name ____________________________________________________________________________

# GIRL FRIENDSHIPS

Every friendship has strengths and difficulties, qualities that feel good and others that feel not so good.

Take some time to consider friendships between girls. Think about your own friendships and about friendships between other girls you know.

Then, with members of your group, brainstorm answers to the following questions. You may have different answers —that's natural and to be expected since every person's experience is unique. Everyone's opinion should be noted and respected.

- List the **strengths** and **things you like** about girls' friendships.

- List the **difficulties** and **things you don't like** about girls' friendships.

- How do these difficulties create disconnections?

Session 3, Handout 1b

Date ____________________

Name ________________________________________________________________

# BOY FRIENDSHIPS

Every friendship has strengths and difficulties, qualities that feel good and others that feel not so good.

Take some time to consider friendships between boys. Think about your own friendships and about friendships between other boys you know.

Then, with members of your group, brainstorm answers to the following questions. You may have different answers — that's natural and to be expected since every person's experience is unique. Everyone's opinion should be noted and respected.

- List the **strengths** and **things you like** about boys' friendships.

- List the **difficulties** and **things you don't like** about boys' friendships.

- How do these difficulties create disconnections?

Session 3, Handout 2

Date ____________________

Name ______________________________________________________________

# Letter of Appreciation

Write a short letter of appreciation to someone you know of the same gender. Let him or her know how much you value the relationship and why. This person could be a friend, a family member, a neighbor, a teacher, a coach, or someone else who matters to you. It's your choice to send the letter or not.

# RECONNECTION

*"Can you help us out? We're in a disconnect."*

## Introduction

*In the last session, we talked in general about connects and disconnects among boys and among girls. Let's start today by considering some of our own relationships.*

## Reflection: Examples of Reconnection

Distribute **Handout 1: Reconnection**.

Read the following directions aloud, giving students time to complete each step before moving on to the next.

1. *Write down the names of up to five people you feel connected to or have felt connected to. These might be friends, classmates, family members, neighbors, teachers... whoever you feel close to right now. You might want to use initials.*
2. *Read over your list and carefully consider your relationship to each person. If you and someone on the list have ever had a disconnect, check (✓) that person's name.*

Ask students to raise their hand if they have a disconnect. Emphasize:

*It looks like disconnects occur in most relationships. Disconnects are bound to happen. When they do, it's important to think about how to move back into connection. I'd like each one of you to have the chance to talk about your own personal experience with reconnection. Let's try this in pairs.*

## Sharing: A Student Exchange and Brainstorm

Ask students to choose a partner or give instructions for pairing them. Instruct partners to brainstorm ten ways people might reconnect. Have them list them on

**Learning Objectives**

Students will:

- Recognize that all relationships involve connections and disconnections
- Demonstrate and list ways to reconnect with another person to strengthen a relationship
- Explain how to move from a relational impasse back into connection
- Discuss why reconnection doesn't often happen instantaneously

**Agenda**

- Introduction
- Reflection: Examples of Reconnection
- Sharing: A Student Exchange and Brainstorm
- Writing: Reconnection Action Steps
- Role-Play: Reconnection

**Materials**

- Handout 1: Reconnection (p 56)

**Handout 1: Reconnection, section 2** (Reconnection Brainstorm). Ask for volunteers to share their responses. Discuss the options with the class. Examples may include:

| | |
|---|---|
| *Reconnects* | *Compromise* |
| *Do something together* | *Talk it out* |
| *Find the underlying problem* | *Forget about it* |
| *Apologize* | *Realize other things are more important* |
| *Give in* | *Take time* |
| *Say sorry without words* | *Let it go* |
| *Make a phone call* | *Have lunch together* |

Pose Question 1 to the class and allow pairs several minutes to answer. Alert students when it is time to trade roles. Then pose Question 2. Remind students to practice active listening.

1. Choose one person from your list with a check (√) by his or her name, someone with whom you've experienced a disconnect. Describe the disconnect to your partner without mentioning the person's name. What happened?
2. If you and this person reconnected, how did it come about? In other words, what did you or the other person say or do? Did anyone else help out? Explain this to your partner.

Ask for volunteers to describe their experiences with disconnects and reconnects. Ask for a volunteer recorder to document on the board examples of actions that led to reconnection. Have the recorder check (√) examples that are duplicated.

## Writing: Reconnection Action Steps

Ask students to consider reconnection from another perspective. Ask them to close their eyes and again to consider the relationships in their lives. Explain:

*This time, however, I want you to think about someone from whom you feel disconnected right now. Consider your friends, classmates, and family members. Is there anyone you are struggling with today? Maybe there's tension and stress in your relationship. Maybe you've had a fight, or a misunderstanding, or exchanged some hard words. Maybe you're not talking at all.*

Ask students to write the person's initials on **Handout 1: Reconnection** in section 3, Personal Reconnection. Underneath, have them list three

### Cultural Consideration

As discussed in Session 2, students from different cultures may have very different ideas about the kinds of behaviors that cause or express disconnects. Because of this, they may be labeled "too sensitive" or "standoffish" by the rest of the class. Example: a high-school student from a high-context culture (see p X) is a member of a study group with three other girls. During the semester, the girls who are from a lower- context culture (see p X) share information and stories about their families, other friends, and boyfriends. At first, the high-context student is uncomfortable, but toward the end of the semester she begins to share her stories also. The semester ends and the girls are in different classes. When they see her in the hallway, the low-context girls wave, but do not stop to talk or call the other girl after school. To the low-context girls, her reluctance to join in their conversations signals that she isn't interested in being friends. Later, when the study group has ended, they relate to her as if she was only an acquaintance—they are happy to see her, but do not feel a strong bond. The high-context student, however, feels she has developed a strong bond with the girls because she has shared personal information with them, which is a sign of trust, something she believes signals the beginning of friendship. When the girls do not continue to spend time with her, she takes it personally, and feels betrayed by them. These kinds of cultural misses happen all the time.

Remind students that we each have different ways of expressing connection, disconnection, and reconnection. Ask them to refrain from judging one another and encourage them to discuss the issues when they get reactions they did not expect. Often these situations arise because of cultural misunderstanding; talking about it can help them accept their differences.

things they could do to strengthen the relationship and work toward better connection.

*Note:* Some students may say that they can't think of anyone. In this case, ask them to try this variation: *Do you know anybody else—a friend, classmate, or family member—who's experiencing a conflict or a disconnect that's affecting you right now? Write down their initials and pretend that you're their coach or trusted advisor. Suggest three things they can do to move toward reconnection.*

## Role-Play: Reconnection

Students use the ideas generated in the previous activity to create original role plays about reconnection.

Review the instructions:

1. *Back in pairs, both of you read aloud your list of three things you might do to move back into connection.*
2. *Together, choose one of your ideas to role-play—verbally or nonverbally—for the class.*
3. *Create a mini role-play about reconnection, using words or not. The emphasis should be on the reconnection, not on the conflict.*

Emphasize that there are times when a relationship cannot be healed, or continue as it was, but people can still remain respectful of each other.

Allow students three or four minutes to create their role-plays. Then ask for volunteers to present their scenes.

Reinforce the importance of reconnection:

> *It's incredible how much we can learn from one another, and how much you already know about how to resolve disconnections. I'm hearing from you that reconnecting can really alter the quality of the relationship. Reconnection can't always happen overnight, though. When a disconnect is major and painful, it may take time to heal, to gain perspective and understanding, to get support, or to figure out the right thing to say or do. Sometimes a disconnection can't be healed. Reconnection is also a huge issue in the world: in politics, foreign policy, diplomacy, and business. These are lifelong learnings that you'll carry into every aspect of your lives.*

### THE TIME FACTOR

Reconnection can't always happen overnight. When a disconnect is major and painful it may take time to heal, to gain perspective and understanding, to get support, or to figure out the right thing to say or do. Sometimes a disconnection can't be healed.

Session 4, Handout 1

Date ____________________

Name ________________________________________________________________

# reconnection

Section 1. CONNECTION/ DISCONNECTION/RECONNECTION

List five people in your life you currently have a connection with. They could be friends, family members, neighbors, teachers, coaches, etc. You may want to use initials.

1.

2.

3.

4.

5.

Read your list again and consider your relationship with each person. If you have had a disconnection with someone on the list in the past, place a check mark next to their name. Now think about what you did to reconnect with each person after you had a disconnection.

Section 2. RECONNECTION BRAINSTORM

List ten ways people can become reconnected.

1.

2.

3.

4.

5.

6.

7.

8.

9.

10.

## Section 3. PERSONAL RECONNECTION

Write the initials of a person with whom you currently feel disconnected.

Think of three ways you could strengthen the relationship with that person and work toward a reconnection.

1.

2.

3.

# GENERATING DIALOGUE

*"Boys and girls want to be able to trust one another. We can really learn a lot from each other."*

## Introduction

*Today we're going to prepare for the Gender Dialogue between girls and boys. Before you can have an open discussion with each other, you first need to figure out what you want to talk about: what you want to understand about each other and what you want members of the other gender to understand about you. Let's encourage each other to be really honest and to include nondominant or minority points of view.*

**Learning Objectives**

Students will:

- Prepare for an open dialogue between girls and boys by generating meaningful questions to members of the other gender
- Discuss what members of the two gender groups think about and are curious to know about each other
- Become more aware of the differences and similarities and connections and disconnections between girls and boys

## Generating Dialogue: Small Groups

Divide the class into small, same-gender groups, optimally three or four per group.

Distribute **Handout 1a: Generating Dialogue-Girls** to the girls and **Handout 1b: Generating Dialogue-Boys** to the boys.

Read the three questions on the handouts to the class.

Allow students fifteen minutes to discuss and answer the three questions. Circulate from group to group and facilitate discussion as needed.

*Note:* If staff is available, it can be helpful for a male teacher to meet with the boys and a female teacher to meet with the girls.

### small groups: a rationale

Some students are reluctant to speak out in front of the whole class, while others tend to dominate. In small groups, everyone has a chance to get involved, to have a say, and to work in close relationship with peers. As a consequence, when the large group recovenes, more students are likely to participate.

## Generating Dialogue: Small-Group Reports

Invite the class back together. Review one question at a time and have a reporter from each group share the group's answers. Choose a volunteer

**Agenda**

- Introduction
- Generating Dialogue: Small Groups
- Generating Dialogue: Small-Group Reports

**Materials**

- Handout 1a: Generating Dialogue-Girls (p 63)
- Handout 1b: Generating Dialogue-Boys (p 64)

**Supporting Activity**

The following activity reinforces the concepts and skills of this session:

- Discussion Blockers (p 93)

to record answers on the board. Alternate between girl and boy reporters for each question.

Sample answers given by students:

| BOYS | GIRLS |
| --- | --- |
| **1. Name 3 strengths that members of the other gender bring to friendships.** | |
| Another point of view | Stress relievers |
| Sensitivity and less violence | Speak their minds |
| Good at communicating | Get over anger quickly |
| Understanding | Lighten things up |
| Peacemakers | Tell you things about other boys |
| Fun to tease | Loyal and steady |
| Understand relationships | Not as emotional |
| Express feelings | |

| BOYS | GIRLS |
| --- | --- |
| **2. What do you most want to understand about members of the other gender group?** | |
| What do girls think about boys? | Why do some boys show off in front of girls? |
| Why do some girls go to the bathroom in groups? | Why are some boys so aggressive? |
| Why do some girls worry so much about their appearance? | What do boys like in girls? |
| Why do some girls take things so personally? | Why do some boys act so macho around their friends? |
| Why are girls so complicated? | Why do some boys wear baggy pants? |
| Why do some girls hug? | Why don't boys cry? |
| Would girls ever use a guy to get close to one of his friends? | Why do some guys think insults are flattering? |
| How do girls think? | Why are some boys obsessed with girls' bodies? |

| Why do girls gossip? | How do boys show their feelings? |
|---|---|
| What do girls do all day? | |

| BOYS | GIRLS |
|---|---|

**3. What do you want members of the other gender to understand about you?**

| | |
|---|---|
| Boys have feelings, too. | Girls do not want to be treated as sex objects. |
| Boys can be friends with girls. | We want you to listen to us and respect us. |
| We're not all totally stuck on your looks. | We are as smart as you. |
| Some guys are bad at taking hints. | We have feelings and don't want to be bossed around. |
| Not all boys like sports. | Boys' opinions can change the way we look at ourselves. |
| We want to succeed. | We are not all alike. |
| We're not weird or smelly. | When we're upset, it's not always related to our hormones. |
| We're under so much pressure to act "cool"! | Please see us for who we really are. |
| Not all boys are romantically interested in girls. | Some of us really love sports. |
| Please see my heart. | Some of us are not interested in boys. |
| We are physical sometimes to let out emotions. | Some of us wound easily. |
| We're under a lot of stress. | We are supposed to act cheerful all the time, but go home and cry. |
| We'd like you to see who we really are. | Most of us are not obsessed with our appearance. |
| We want to be your friend. | We are just like you, but not just like you. |

## Cultural Considerations

Cultural stereotypes often have gender-specific references. Students may deal with these by asking questions like, "Why do Latino boys always..."? Or, "Is it true that Asian girls..."? (The ethnicities named are only examples; any group might be substituted.) Students may be attempting to explore their cultural differences. Open up the conversation to explore those differences without allowing students to stereotype one another. If stereotypes do surface, make the students aware that there are people within that group who do not fit the stereotype and there are also people who are not a part of that group who do exhibit those behaviors. The problem with stereotypes is that they assign a certain behavior to one group and allow others to make judgments about members of that group based upon the stereotype.

**Note:** Before Session 6, type up student responses to all three questions. Make a copy for each class member. At the start of Session 6, students will use this sheet as the foundation for the gender dialogue.

Date ____________________

Name ________________________________________________________________

# Generating Dialogue: Girls

Have fun discussing and answering the following three questions with members of your group. You'll probably each have different and interesting ideas to contribute. Everyone's ideas matter and should be noted.

Choose one person to be the group reporter, to write down answers and report to the rest of the class. Remember: the reporter will report group answers **without** identifying the specific person who said the answer, so here's your chance to be really honest!

1. Name at least three strengths that boys bring to friendships with girls.

2. What do you **most** want to understand and know about boys? (Write down as many questions as you want.)

3. What do you **most** want boys to understand and know about **you**? (Write down as many questions as you want.)

Session 5, Handout 1b Date ____________________

Name ____________________________________________

# Generating Dialogue: Boys

Have fun discussing and answering the following three questions with members of your group. You'll probably each have different and interesting ideas to contribute. Everyone's ideas matter and should be noted.

Choose one person to be the group reporter, to write down answers and report to the rest of the class. Remember: the reporter will report group answers **without** identifying the specific person who said the answer, so here's your chance to be really honest!

1. Name at least three strengths that girls bring to friendships with boys.

2. What do you **most** want to understand and know about girls? (Write down as many questions as you want.)

3. What do you **most** want girls to understand and know about **you**? (Write down as many questions as you want.)

# GENDER DIALOGUE

*"Everything I learned in the gender dialogue was important. We really have a lot to learn from each other."*

## Introduction

**Note:** Before beginning this session, take time to review and become comfortable with the suggestions for facilitating a successful dialogue on page 68.

Welcome students to the dialogue and offer some simple words of encouragement:

> *Today we're going to have a cross-gender dialogue between boys and girls. You'll get to talk and listen and learn about each other—from each other. The purpose is to come to a greater understanding of each other, of differences and similarities, so that connection between boys and girls can be strengthened.*

## Generating Dialogue: Ground Rules

Have boys and girls sit in two separate semicircles, facing each other. The teacher/ leader should sit in the circle at the juncture between the boys and girls.

Ask students to clarify the difference between debate and dialogue.

> *In a debate, people square off* against *one another. Differences in ideas and perspectives are used to defend our own positions and find flaws in another's position. The goal of a debate is to win! The goal of a dialogue is totally different: we talk* together *to build understanding. Different perspectives lead to greater awareness and sense of community. Today, we're going to dialogue.*

Quickly review ground rules.

- Everyone participates.
- One person speaks at a time.
- Be honest and nonjudgmental.

**Learning Objectives**

Students will:

- Engage in a dialogue about difference that moves beyond superficial assumptions toward greater understanding and connection
- Realize that mutual understanding and connection is possible between girls and boys

**Agenda**

- Introduction
- Generating Dialogue: Ground Rules
- Generating Dialogue: Questions 1 and 2
- Generating Dialogue: The Gender Dialogue
- Generating Dialogue: Question 3
- Summing Up

**Materials**

- Background for Teachers/Leaders: Facilitating Dialogue (p 68)
- Dialogue Example (p 69)
- Handout 1: from Session 5 (Note: The teacher/leader will need to prepare this ahead of time by typing re-

sponses recorded from the previous session)

**Supporting Activities**

The following activities reinforce the concepts and skill of this session:

- Understanding Culture (p 94)
- What Makes Conflict Escalate (p 94)
- Going Up the Escalator (p 95)
- Going Down CAPS (p 96)

- Raise your hand if you want to answer or ask a question.
- Disagreements are okay, but not disrespect.
- Use the phrases "*some* boys" and "*some* girls."
- Listen to what each person has to say before responding.
- If you don't understand something, ask for an explanation.
- Call others (and yourself) on joking that disrupts dialogue.
- No names! Refer to people generally: "I know *a boy* who..."

## Generating Dialogue: Questions 1 and 2

Pass out sheets of student responses from Session 5.

*Last session you came up with great insights and questions. Let's take a minute to review these now and move from there into dialogue.*

Ask for a volunteer from one gender group to read the list of their gender group's answers to Question 1. Follow with a volunteer from the other gender group. Discuss. Repeat with Question 2 and proceed with dialogue.

*Note:* Students will revisit Question 3 at the end of the dialogue. Be sure to allow at least ten minutes at the end of the session to review Question 3 and to sum up.

### Dialogue "Disconnects"

Students may ask inappropriate questions or make impolite comments. Underlying such indiscretions is often a valid wish for information. Help students by directing them to more "connecting" language: "What do you really want to know?" or "Could you ask that in a more respectful way?" or "Can you state that in a more connecting way?" By asking questions like these, you model a way toward reconnection for students to emulate.

## Generating Dialogue: The Gender Dialogue

Remind students that an important goal is equal participation between girls and boys.

Review dialogue protocol:

1. *We'll flip a coin to see who begins. After that, questions will go back and forth between girls and boys.*
2. *Anyone can volunteer to ask a question. Ask anything you want—a question from the sheet or a brand new one.*
3. *Anyone in the other gender group can volunteer to respond to a question.*

Join in, as needed, to facilitate the flow of conversation. See Facilitating Dialogue (p 68) for suggestions. The dialogue may require active facilitation and encouragement at the start. Students commonly become more at ease, and the conversation grows, after the first question or two.

If the dialogue is still going strong at the end of class, consider extending it into a second session. A second dialogue may be especially valuable if the group feels disconnected or if further discussion is intensely requested. Note, however, that the dialogue may not have the same momentum the next time students meet.

## Generating Dialogue: Question 3

During the last ten minutes of the dialogue, ask students to refer to **Handout 1: Responses from Session 5** and their answers to Question 3: "What do you most want members of the other gender to understand about *you*?" Ask for a girl and boy volunteer to read aloud the two lists of answers. Continue the dialogue and ask students about how they feel and what they have observed.

## Summing Up

Take a moment to sum up key points of the dialogue, to affirm students' participation, and to express appreciation for the group's work. Point out key moments of connection, disconnection, or reconnection during the session.

### Include All Voices

The leaders should always stay attuned to facilitating the expression of minority or non-dominant perspectives. In one group, one girl strongly stated, "It's really different in my culture, we tell them what to do." A boy from the same culture playfully responded, "that's what we have to deal with." A respectful discussion of cultural differences then began. One girl stated that "women in my family are very strong too." Another girl concluded, "In some cultures no matter how successful a woman is, she is valued by the man she is with."

# BACKGROUND FOR TEACHERS/LEADERS

## Facilitating Dialogue

The gender dialogue takes place between boys and girls, with adults actively facilitating the process. Your role is that of an active guide to help navigate a safe, fair, and authentic dialogue—one that moves beyond stereotypes, deepens understanding and empathy, and fosters a sense of the *We*—for all involved. Aim to help individual students speak up and clarify ideas and to guide the group as a whole to a more strongly connected place.

Here are some ways to facilitate these goals:

**Invite individual participation.** Keep track of the students who are not participating and invite them into the conversation.

**Cultivate an inclusive atmosphere.** Facilitate an expression of differences that may be related to race, class, ethnicity, sexual orientation, or physical ability, etc. In addition to issues of diversity, students often experience differences of power within the social order of their school. In every group, there are always people who do not feel ready or safe enough yet to express differences. Be aware and sensitive to this and assure students that all perspectives are welcome and important.

**Identify questions that everyone might answer.** If you think a question is particularly relevant to the group or that both boys and girls hold a range of opinions on a particular topic, you may request that every member of a gender group respond to a given question: "Let's go around the circle and give every boy/girl the chance to speak." Leaders should always remain attuned to cultural differences and encourage respectful expression of those differences.

**Don't let an uneasy comment stand.** Invite kids to investigate further. For instance, "I sense that comment is a little difficult for some girls. Is this correct? Would any girl like to say more?"

**Help students dialogue through uncomfortable moments.** When conversation takes a difficult turn, don't be surprised if students exhibit such disconnection strategies as joking, minimizing the topic, or changing the subject. Help students stay with the topic; this may well be an important growing edge. "This stuff *is* hard, but we can get through it together. We'll all be better off if we stay in the dialogue."

**Call for a questioning of inaccuracies.** If a girl makes a mistaken assumption, for example, you might say, "Does that sound right to you boys? Or to *some* of you?" Or perhaps there's a divergence of opinion among girls: "Does *every* girl think the same on this one?"

**Keep the focus on respect.** Ask students to rephrase off-putting questions or comments in more "connecting" language.

**Balance seriousness and fun.** The tone can be light, humorous, and fun as long as it supports healthy connection in the group.

**Direct kids to talk to each other.** Encourage them to "speak to the group."

**Ask students to rephrase generalizations.** A girl asks, "Why do boys always want to be macho?" Ask for a modification: "Why do *some* boys want to be macho?"

**Help students shape or clarify questions.** A boy asks, "Why do some girls get so upset at such little things?" You might ask him, "Can you get more specific or give an example?"

**Monitor the pace; keep it moving.** If conversation starts to lag or become repetitive on a given topic, call for a new question.

**Help deepen the discussion.** When you think greater understanding is possible on a given topic, you might say, "I sense there might be *more* to what the girls are saying. This sounds really important. Do any boys sense this too?"

**Reinforce important points.** There's no need to comment on every student response, but if you'd like students to think more consciously about a given point, repeat the point to the class and invite further conversation. For instance, "So, we're hearing from boys that sometimes roughhousing is a way to connect. We're *also* hearing that sometimes it *isn't* playful, it's about exerting power over somebody else."

**Help move the group through discomfort.** If, for example, students start giggling after a boy poses a question about PMS (premenstrual syndrome), point out that sometimes people laugh when they feel uncomfortable. "Even though this is a sensitive question, it would probably be really helpful for the boys to understand what the girls experience."

**Strive for balanced "airtime."** Alternate questions between gender groups. If either group monopolizes commentary, invite feedback from the other.

**Encourage mutual empathy.** For instance, if a boy describes an incident of being judged by a girl, you might ask, "Do you think *girls* ever feel that way too? Would any girl like to comment?"

**Stay open to different perspectives.** Notice any judgments or assumptions of your own that may be operating.

**If a particular group is very polarized and unable to work through anger**, see the Supplementary Activities suggested on page X.

## Close-Up: A Gender Dialogue Example

The following excerpts are from dialogues that took place after students had brainstormed answers to the questions: What strengths do members of the other gender group bring to relationships? What do you most want to understand about members of the other gender? What do you most want members of the other gender to understand about you? The first is from a dialogue between seventh graders, the second between high school juniors.

**Seventh Grade**

A girl asks a boy, "Why do you act one way when you're with me and another when you're with your friends?"

"Because when I'm with my friends," the boy says, "I have to act cool."

"We just wish the boys could be themselves."

A second boy speaks up. "How can girls show their feelings to each other so easily?"

"We tell each other everything," a second girl says. "We are, like, really close."

"If you tell a girl you're feeling bad, she'll help you," another girl adds. "Why are some boys so afraid of showing their feelings anyway?"

The boys pause. Some fidget with their hands.

"I see a lot of girls nodding their heads," says the adult leader. "They really want to know what you think. Anyone want to begin?"

"We only cry when something really important happens," a boy explains. "Like when my dog died."

**High School Juniors**

A male student says, "Why do some girls go for the popular macho types who treat them so badly?" One female student answers, "Some of us go for social status, just like some of you."

A second female student answers, "Maybe it's like an expression of low self-esteem."

After a pause, another male student asks, "Do all of you agree with that?"

A third female student says, "I actually don't know why. It's really stupid."

A fourth female says thoughtfully, "I think we like the chase, too. But for us...you hope you are going to be the one who gets him finally to open his heart." A fifth female says, "Most girls really like boys who treat them well."

# CELEBRATING THE "WE"

*"It takes everybody's working together to build the class 'We.' It is what we all want and like. It's a sense of belonging."*

## Introduction

Arrange chairs in a circle to create a sense of continuity with the last session.

Invite students into the circle. Students can sit where they choose.

> *This is our final session. Today we're going to celebrate this class, our group "We." Throughout these sessions, and especially in the gender dialogue, you've all shown an ability to learn together. Let's reflect together on what we've learned.*

## Sharing: Celebrating the "We"

On the board, write: "Tell us one thing about how this group has changed for you over the course of the sessions. Was there a certain idea or moment that really surprised or moved you?"

Go around the circle and ask each student if he or she would like to share.

Teachers/leaders can participate and speak about their experience with this class as a community.

**Note*: If you are planninng on using any or all of the optional sessions, you may want to do them first and close with Session 7.

**Learning Objectives**

Students will:

- Name and understand experiences of the "We."
- Recognize and appreciate how much they've learned and how the group has grown together over the course of the sessions.

**Agenda**

- Introduction
- Sharing: Celebrating the "We"
- Brainstorm: Getting Real
- Writing: Reflection
- Go-Round: Sharing the Learning

**Materials**

- Handout 1: Sharing the Learning (p 75)
- A box for collecting student handouts
- A celebratory treat: e.g. cookies, pretzels, etc., napkins

## Brainstorm: Getting Real

Invite students to explore the complexities of applying this knowledge in the real world:

> *Of course, it's one thing to* know *the right things to do to build connection and another thing to actually* do *them. Let's talk about what gets in the way of building connection—here and now in our day-to-day lives.*

Pose the following three questions to the class. Ask for a volunteer to compile lists of answers on the board.

1. *What can prevent a person—or a group of people—from connecting when we all know so many ways to do this? What gets in the way?*
2. *What can we do to get through obstacles that interfere with building a "We"?*
3. *What makes it difficult to transfer knowledge into action?*

Summarize the importance of identifying stumbling blocks to connection.

> *Each one of us is learning and in process—along with leaders, communities, and nations across the world—when it comes to practicing connection. When we can look at and talk about what gets in the way as we've been doing together these past weeks, then we have a real chance at doing things differently— changing ourselves, our relationships, or working together to change the world.*

### WHAT GETS IN THE WAY

All of us often know and can voice the "right" answers. Translating knowledge into practice can be difficult, requiring a different set of skills and the availability of support. Acknowledge the discrepancy between "knowing" and "doing" and how hard it can be to put into practice what we know.

## Writing: Reflection

Distribute **Handout 1: Sharing the Learning** to each student. Allow students five minutes to complete it. Explain that handwriting should be clear because students will be reading each other's writing.

Place the cardboard box in the middle of the circle. When students are finished, direct them to fold their handouts in half and place them in the box.

## Go-Round: Sharing the Learning

Pass the box around the circle. Have each student draw one handout from the box. If anyone pulls his or her own sheet, she/he can draw again.

Pose aloud the first question on the handout. Then, without pausing for discussion or comments, go around the circle, having each student read the response on her/his handout. Encourage students to listen actively.

After the go-round on Question 1, pause for a brief discussion of any common themes, surprises, or important learnings.

Repeat the go-round and discussion for Question 2 and 3 and 4.

After Question 4, pass the basket of food around the circle with a sense of ritual to celebrate and affirm the "*We.*"

Sample student responses:

**1. What are the most important things you've learned about relationships between girls and boys?**

We can/should be good friends.

Boys bring things to a friendship that girls can't.

Without a boy/girl friendship, you're missing out.

There are many assumptions and clichés about relationships we must ignore.

Boys need to learn from girls about expressing feelings.

We need to get beyond stereotypes and fears about each other.

We can really hurt each other if we don't listen.

**2. What happens if we don't build the "We" in a classroom/school?**

People won't feel comfortable around each other.

No one will share feelings.

Our discussions will be much more superficial.

People will be afraid to be themselves.

Conflicts might go underground or lead to fights.

People won't be able to ask the group for help.

People might get hurt.

Much less learning will take place.

**3. What gets in the way of building a "We"?**

Fear.

Habit.

Fear of being put down, laughed at, or being the only one.

## 4. What does it take to build a group "We'?

No laughing at or making fun of others.

Trust, cooperation, and respect.

Courage.

Eagerness to learn from one another.

The faith we have in each other.

Exploring diversity.

Shared values.

Knowing you are supported by others.

Time to learn to work together.

Commitment.

Dealing directly with conflicts and disconnects.

Session 7, Handout 1

Date ____________________

Name ______________________________________________________________

# SHARING THE LEARNING

Take a few minutes to reflect upon what you've learned in this course. Your answers will be read by someone else—in the spirit of sharing our learning.

1. What are the most important things you've learned about relationships between girls and boys?

2. What happens if we don't build the "We" in a classroom/school?

3. What can get in the way of building a "We"?

4. What does it take to build a group "We"?

# THE MEDIA: STEREOTYPES AND DISCONNECTS

*"I learned that advertising really does have an impact on us."*

## Brainstorm: Gender Images in Teen Magazines

Divide the class into same-gender groups of three to five students. Have teen magazines ready. Be sure the magazines represent many cultures and types of teens. Ask students to imagine they are from "another planet," and they have no knowledge of gender differences on earth.

Distribute **Handout 1a: Gender Images and the Media** (for girls) and **1b: Gender Images and the Media** (for boys).

Give students 10- 15 minutes to complete the handout.

## Sharing: Discussing Gender Images in Teen Magazines

Resume the large-group format. Have a reporter from each group record the group's answers on the board for discussion. Discuss the answers as a large group.

When the discussion is finished, ask students to think about how the media shapes images of relationships. Ask: What does the media show as being "cool" in relationships? What would you say is "cool" in relationships?

**Learning Objectives**

Students will:

- Become aware of the dominant cultural messages from the media about boys/girls and relationships
- Understand how the media shapes standards of what's "cool," valuable, and attractive
- Understand how these standards are expressed by media icons (movies, music, TV, models)

**Agenda**

- Brainstorm: Gender Images in Teen Magazines
- Sharing: Discussing Gender Images in Teen Magazines

**Materials**

- Ten teen magazines
- Handout 1a: Gender Images and the Media (for girls) (p 78)
- Handout 1b: Gender Images and the Media (for boys) (p 79)

Optional Session A, Handout 1a

Date ____________________

Name ____________________________________________________________

# Gender Images and the Media—Girls

**Directions**: You come from another planet and all you have to rely on for information about male and female genders is from these teen magazines. Answer questions 1-7. Reflect on and discuss questions.

1. List five qualities of femininity that are generated through the teen magazine.

2. How do the media's images affect girls and their relationships with each other?

3. What are the images of masculinity and how do you think these images affect boys?

4. How do the media's images of boy/girl relationships affect girls both positively and negatively?

5. What relationships are missing? What effect does that have on attitudes about relationships?

6. List three ways of resisting these stereotypical images.

7. How can we encourage the media to use healthy gender images?

Optional Session A, Handout 1b

Date ______________________

Name ________________________________________________________________

# Gender Images and the Media—Boys

**Directions**: You come from another planet and all you have to rely on for information about male and female genders is from these teen magazines. Answer questions 1-7. Reflect on and discuss questions.

1. List five qualities of masculinity that are generated through the teen magazine.

2. How do the media's images affect boys and their relationships with each other?

3. What are the images of femininity and how do you think these images affect girls?

4. How do the media's images of boy/girl relationships affect boys both positively and negatively?

5. What relationships are missing? What effect does that have on attitudes about relationships?

6. List three ways of resisting these stereotypical images.

7. How can we encourage the media to use healthy gender images?

# "GOING OUT": QUALITIES OF HEALTHY AND UNHEALTHY RELATIONSHIPS

*"Everyone knows someone who has tried 'hooking up' through the Internet."*

## Background Information for Teacher/Leader

There are many different ways of "going out" or dating—different stages, different preferences. Not everyone dates. Not everyone is heterosexual, but dominant images in our school and in the media about what "cool" relationships look like impact us all. Most kids feel pressured to conform to these dominant images. These images don't necessarily reflect either our values or what is healthy.

**Learning Objectives**

Students will:

- Understand qualities that define healthy relationships
- List the "red flags" that warn boys/girls of unhealthy relationships

**Agenda**

- Brainstorm: Qualities of a Relationship

**Materials**

- Handout 1: Relationship Questions (p 83)

## Brainstorm: Qualities of a Relationship

Divide students into small, same-gender groups and distribute **Handout 1: Relationship Questions**. Before groups answer the questions, have students close their eyes and talk them through this visualization and questions.

> *Picture a healthy dating relationship. Take your time and notice what images come to your mind. Choose one relationship. What qualities do you admire? Now visualize a relationship in your school. What stands out for you that you admire? What stands out for you that you don't like? Do you feel pressure to act or look a particular way in your relationships? If so, how? What qualities are important to you in a dating relationship?"*

Give groups 10-15 minutes to answer the questions on the handout.

Have a reporter from each group share the results. Discuss the qualities students have listed about healthy and unhealthy relationships and how people can support each other and increase their ability to make healthy choices.

Sample Answers:

| Qualities of a Healthy Relationship | Red Flags of a Unhealthy Relationship |
|---|---|
| Support | Want power and control over other |
| Trust | Jealousy |
| Honesty | Dishonesty, lack of trust |
| Can say what's on your mind | Blaming |
| Caring | Possessive, controlling |
| Affectionate | Degrading sexual comments |
| Mutual respect | Can't talk about problems |
| Notice each other's feelings | Flirting with others |
| Healthy conflict | Abusive fighting |

*Note:* Have middle-school students speak about commonalities in their responses, gender stereotypes, and pressures they may feel about relationships. Have them also speak about ways they could be more aware of these stereotypical messages and ways they might resist the pressures.

*Note:* Have high-school students speak about commonalities and differences that emerged from the brainstorm. Emphasis can be on how can we work together to resist pressures that interfere with healthy relationships? What can the group or community do together?

Date ______________

Name ______________

# Relationship Questions

**Directions**: Answer the following questions.

1. List the qualities of healthy relationships.

2. List the qualities or "red flags" of unhealthy relationships.

3. How can we support each other and increase our ability to make healthy relationship choices?

4. What actions can you take if you find yourself or another in an abusive relationship?

5. What can the group or community do to support healthy relationships?

# THE IMPACT OF DRUGS AND ALCOHOL ON RELATIONSHIPS*

*"I feel like I'm supposed to drink and be 'cool' to get a popular girl to look at me."*

## Discussion: Statistics

Distribute **Handout 1: Statistics**.

Present the statistics concerning adolescent and alcohol use, abuse, and addiction, and their impact on student development, behavior, and contribution to unhealthy/abusive relationships. Have students discuss the statistics in comparison to their personal observations. Ask: *Does this reflect your own experience and observations accurately? Do you think this reflects our community?*

## Brainstorm: Drugs and Alcohol and Relationships

Divide students into small same-gender groups. Distribute **Handout 2a: Drugs and Alcohol Use** (girls) to the girls and **Handout 2b: Drugs and Alcohol Use** (boys) to the boys. Give groups 10 minutes to complete the questions.

Ask a reporter from each group to share their group's answers with the class.

**Learning Objectives**

Students will:

- Discuss the impact of drug and alcohol use on individual development, decision-making, and relationships

**Agenda**

- Discussion: Statistics

**Materials**

- Handout 1: Statistics (p 86)
- Handout 2a: Drug and Alcohol Use-Girls (p 87)
- Handout 2b: Drug and Alcohol Use-Boys (p 88)

**Note*: Teachers should decide on the appropriateness of this lesson for middle-school students.

Date ____________________

Name ______________________________________________________________

# STATISTICS

First use of alcohol typically begins around the age of 13.

Binge drinking is having five or more drinks of alcohol in a row. About 14% of eighth-grade students report binge drinking during the past two weeks. One in four (26%) tenth-grade students report binge drinking in the past two weeks.

The brain does not finish developing until a person is around 21. Alcohol use at an early age can affect memory, ability to learn, and ability to make good judgements.

Nearly 90% of tenth graders and 75% of eighth graders think alcohol is "fairly easy" or "very easy" to get.

Both preteens and teens say their main sources of information about drugs and alcohol are entertainment media, television, movies, and music.

Alcohol abuse is linked to as many as two-thirds of all sexual assaults and date rapes of teens and college students.

Binge drinkers and drug users are three times more likely to contract an STD.

In addition to alcoholism, other behaviors linked to early age of first drink are drug abuse, delinquency, antisocial behavior in adulthood, and decline in academic achievement.

An intoxicated person at the wheel of a car is a lethal weapon.

Underage drinking is a factor in nearly half of all teen automobile crashes, the leading cause of death among teenagers.

Statistics referenced from *Words Can Work, When Talking with Kids about Alcohol*, by Jean Blake, BlakeWorks, 2003.

Date ____________________

Name ________________________________________________________________

# Drug and Alcohol Use—Girls

**Directions**: Answer the following questions.

1. How do media stereotypes contribute to why and how girls use drugs or alcohol?

2. How does the media present male/female relationships in relation to drug and alcohol use?

3. How does drug or alcohol use affect decision-making in dating relationships? How might this contribute to developing an unhealthy or abusive relationship?

4. How can we support each other in resisting unhealthy messages and making healthy choices?

5. How can schools, families, and communities support students in making healthy choices?

Date ____________________

Name ____________________________________________________________

# Drug and Alcohol Use—Boys

**Directions**: Answer the following questions.

1. How do media stereotypes contribute to why and how boys use drugs or alcohol?

2. How does the media present male/female relationships in relation to drug and alcohol use?

3. How does drug or alcohol use affect decision-making in dating relationships? How might this contribute to developing an unhealthy or abusive relationship?

4. How can we support each other in resisting unhealthy messages and making healthy choices?

5. How can schools, families, and communities support students in making healthy choices?

# SUPPORTING ACTIVITIES

## Activity A: Diagramming the "We"

Distribute **Handout A1: "Who Are We?"** (p 98) to each student. Have students fill in circles, one at a time.

1. "Who am *I* in this class?" In the first circle, students list their strengths and difficulties.
2. "Who are *others* in this classroom?" Students list strengths and difficulties of others in class *without using names*. Direct students to use the phrase "**some** students" to avoid stereotyping.
3. "Who are *We*?" Students describe the class as a whole in general terms.

Ask students to read their descriptions of the class "We." Appreciate similarities and differences in their answers.

Example:

**Who am I in this class?**

☺

I listen. I contribute.
I respect others' opinions.

☹

I'm shy. Sometimes I really disagree with what other people are saying.

**Who are others in this class?**

Some people are respectful and understanding.
Some people listen when I am talking during discussion.

Some people talk too much and don't listen or care when others are talking.

**Who are *We*?**

Overall, most people want to learn and are respectful, helpful, and caring.

## Activity B: Class Mission

"Who are *we* as a class? Who do *we* want to be as a class? What's our overall purpose and vision as a group?" Have students brainstorm a list of answers and formulate a class purpose statement.

Students can create a poster with the class statement and display in a prominent place.

## Activity C: Class Quilt: Representing the "We"

Hand out a square of colored paper to each student. Using colored pencils, markers, paint, glitter, etc., have students decorate squares to represent something significant about themselves: e.g., a favorite activity, color, accomplishment, etc.

Have students present their square to the class.

Assemble squares into a class quilt and display it in the room.

## Activity D: Characteristics of Active Listening

Explain that good listening requires active participation. Ask students what good listening looks like and what it sounds like. Write their answers on the board in the form of a T-chart, listing the attending skills (nonverbal ways of showing a person is listening) and responding skills (verbal responses) that make up active listening:

**ACTIVE LISTENING**

| What You See (Attending Skills) | What You Hear (Responding Skills) |
|---|---|
| Eye contact with the speaker | Verbal encouragers like "Uh, huh," "Tell me more," and "Yeah" |
| Leaning forward or nodding | Agreeing with something the person has said |
| Sitting still, no fidgeting or playing with stuff | Restating what the speaker says |
| No interrupting | Reflecting what the speaker is feeling |
| Attentive silence; giving a person time to respond | Asking open-ended questions like "What happened?" or "How did you feel about that?" |

Distribute **Handout D1: Active Listening Practice** (p 99).

Have each student find a partner and practice active-listening skills. Each person gets two minutes to speak. While one partner is speaking, the other practices active-listening techniques. Suggestions for topics:

- an experience that made them feel they were treated unfairly
- something a family member does that really bothers them
- a rule at school that they think is unfair
- a time they did something that they are proud of

## Activity E: Observation Sheet: How Are "We"?

Ask one or several students to act as observers for a class period. For a specified time period (e.g., one class) observers take note of "connecting"and "disconnecting" behaviors in the entire classroom or within a small group.

Give each observer a copy of **Handout E1: Observation Sheet: How are "We"?** (p 100) Review the lists of "connecting" and "disconnecting" behaviors with the class. Can students think of additional behaviors to add to either list?

At the end of the class period, have observers report to the class, speaking in general terms without naming names. For example, "I noticed fifteen examples of connecting behaviors in class today. One student offered to help another with her handout, etc."

As a variation, distribute Observation Sheets to everyone in the class and ask students to observe and keep track of their own "connecting" and "disconnecting" behaviors during a class period or over the course of a week.

## Activity F: Community Survey

Distribute **Handout F1: Community Survey** (p 101) at any time to get a measure of students' sense of community in the classroom. Have each student fill out a survey sheet.

Emphasize that there are no right answers. Report the class averages.

Reflection questions:

1. What do the class averages tell us about our community?
2. What can we do to help build the "We"?

## Activity G: Stereotypes

Ask students to find partners. In each pair, one person says, "Adults are ...," and the other person responds with whatever comes into his or her head. Repeat this ten times, then switch roles.

Write "Adults are..." on the board. Define *stereotype* (an oversimplified generalization about a particular group, race, or gender; usually derogatory). Ask students to volunteer some of the answers they and their partners came up with, and list them on the board. Go over the list to see which of the responses might be stereotypes. Ask, "Can you think of a real person or a story that counters this stereotype?"

Many people have stereotypes about young people. Ask the class to think of as many of these as they can. List students' responses on the board.

Discuss:

- How do these stereotypes make you feel?
- Does it matter if we stereotype people?
- What effects do such stereotypes have?
- Do they restrict people in some way? How?

## Activity H: Discussion Blockers

Before class, choose a topic for a class discussion that you know students have a strong opinion about. Ask nine students to exhibit poor listening skills during the discussion. Assign each of them a discussion blocker from the list. Ask these students to wait two or three minutes into the student-led discussion before they begin saying their blocker statements.

**Discussion Blockers**

- **Distracting/avoiding**: Change the subject.
- **Criticizing**: Criticize what the last person said.
- **Interrupting**: Interrupt the person who is talking.
- **Being sarcastic**: Make a sarcastic comment about what has been said: "Oh, please! Like that would ever work!"
- **"Yes, but" statements**: Begin your point with "Yes, but" and always contradict what the other person just said.
- **Lecturing/moralizing**: Lecture the group on what they *should* think or do.
- **Blaming**: Blame a type of individual for causing the problem.
- **Attacking questions**: Use an intimidating tone. Suggest that you doubt the speaker's sincerity.
- **Having all the answers**: Try to solve the problem for everyone else. Insist your solution is the best.

Begin the activity by asking students to think about why we listen. Sample answers:

- to get instructions
- to understand another person's feelings and point of view
- to help others
- to learn about others and the world around us
- to be entertained

Lead the discussion.

Ask the students to make note of how the discussion on the chosen topic proceeds and how they communicate with each other. After about ten minutes, stop the discussion. Ask students to identify the communication blockers they heard and how those blockers affected the discussion. Write the communication blockers on the board and discuss them.

## Activity I: Understanding Culture

Divide students into groups of three or four. Give each student two minutes to tell something about his or her background, addressing the following (be sure to signal each time two minutes has elapsed):

- Where were your birth and/or adoptive grandparents and/or parents born?
- What is your birth and/or adoptive cultural background?
- What is an important value that your family has that they have communicated to you?
- How are gender differences seen in your cultural framework?

Bring the class back together for a discussion of the following questions:

- What did you notice about diversity as you did this activity?
- How did it feel to talk about aspects of your culture in particular?

Ask volunteers to share what their cultural group is and the value that is important to them. Write the name of cultural groups and the values described on the board or on chart paper. When a cultural group or value is repeated, place a check next to the phrase to see how often a particular value comes up.

Discussion:

- To what degree are there similarities in the values listed?
- How can we account for some of the differences in family values listed?
- How do you suppose these family values came about?
- What do these values tell us about particular ethnic or cultural groups?

## Activity J: What Makes Conflict Escalate?

Introduce the term *escalate*, relating it to *escalator*. Explain that when a conflict gets worse, we say that it escalates. Draw an escalator on the board as follows:

As you draw the escalator, explain that each step on the escalator is a behavior on

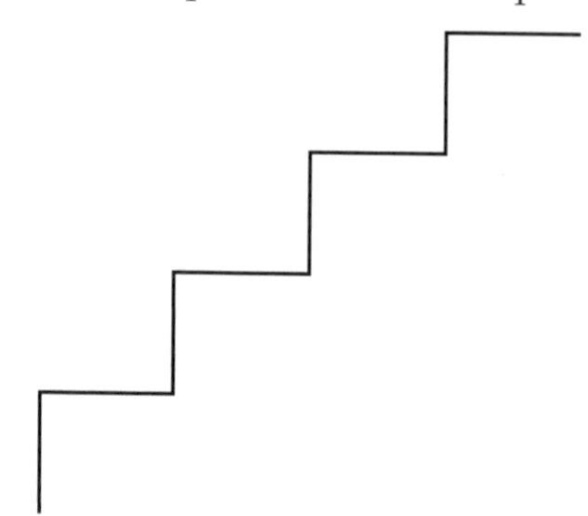

the part of the people in the conflict that makes the conflict worse.

Distribute one of the skits from **Handout J1: What Makes Conflict Escalate Skit** (p 102)for volunteers to perform. Next, ask the class to identify the first step on the escalator, the second step, and so on. Write each step on the escalator you drew on the board. Continue until you reach the top of the escalator.

Review each step on the escalator and ask the class: What do you think the person was feeling at this step on the escalator? Write their responses underneath the step. There may be more than one feeling for a particular step. Emphasize that it is not just behavior that escalates during a conflict. Feelings also escalate. In fact, you could say feelings are the energy source that pushes up the conflict escalator.

Circle the top step and present the following:

> *The higher you go on the escalator, the harder it is to come down. The top of any conflict escalator is the place where the people in the conflict get into trouble, or walk away in a huff, or say they'll never speak to each other again, or get violent. In an international conflict, the top of the escalator is where wars happen. You can get down from the top of the escalator, but it's hard. Try not to go to the top of the escalator!*

Discussion:

- When you're in a conflict, how do feelings affect the way you behave?
- What feelings most often come up for you in conflicts?
- How do feelings escalate as the conflict escalates?
- What examples have you seen of conflicts escalating?

## Activity K: Going Up the Conflict Escalator

Explain to students:

- Every behavior in the conflict is either a step up or a step down the conflict escalator.
- Behavior that makes the conflict worse will take it another step up the escalator.
- Every step up the conflict escalator has feelings that go with it. As the conflict escalates, so do the feelings.
- The higher you go on the escalator, the harder it is to come down.

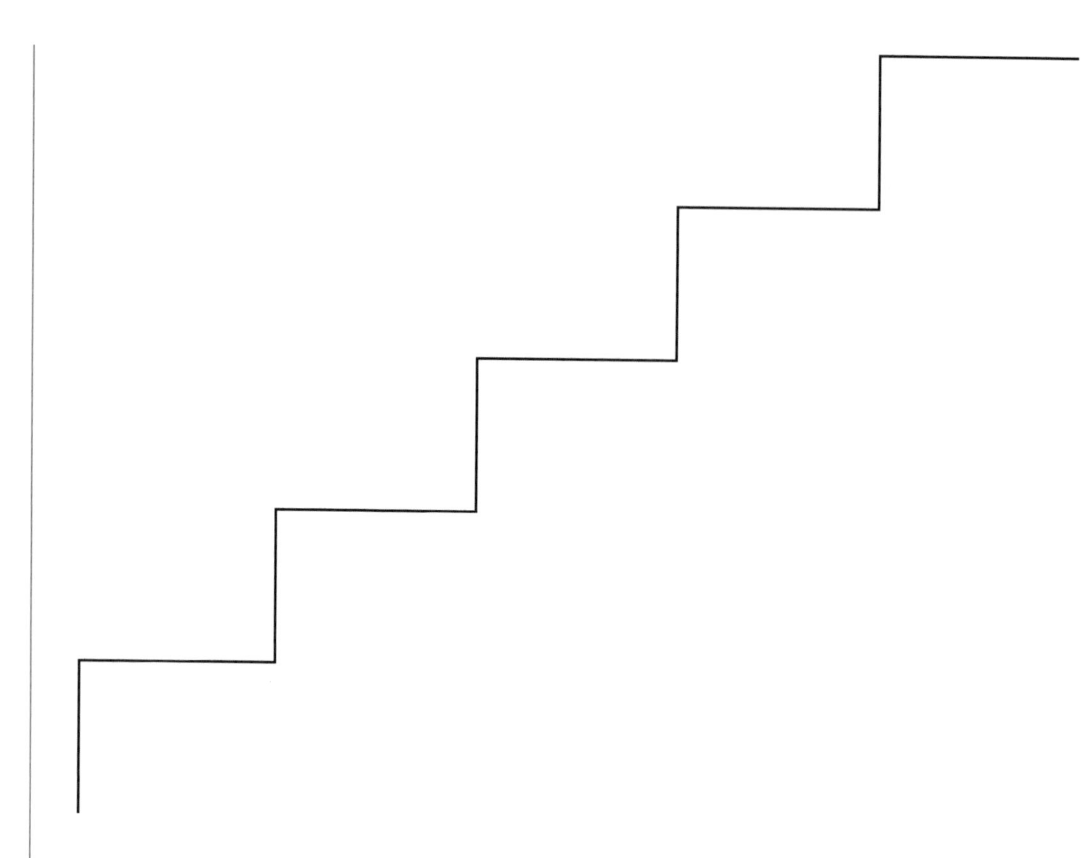

## Activity L: Going Down the Conflict Escalator- CAPS

Review the meaning of the conflict escalator: as conflicts get worse, they escalate, which is like going up to the top of an escalator. In order to resolve conflict, we have to get it to come down the escalator. This is called de-escalating the conflict.

Draw an Up escalator and then add four steps down. Using this diagram give the following mini-lecture to explain CAPS:

> *There is a formula for coming down the escalator that is called CAPS. (Label the Down steps C, A, P, S.) These letters stand for* **C***alm Down,* **A***gree to Work It Out,* **P***oint of View on the Problem, and* **S***olve the Problem.*
>
> *The first step down the escalator is Calm Down, because no one can resolve a conflict if they are furious. The second step is Agree to Work It Out, because it would be almost impossible to come up with a mutually agreeable solution if one of the people in the conflict refused to try to work it out. Third, the two people need to share their perspective or Point of View on the Problem. Fourth, once they agree on what conflict they are trying to solve, they Solve the Problem in a way that leads to a mutually agreeable solution, or as close to one as possible.*

Read the following conflict situation to the class:

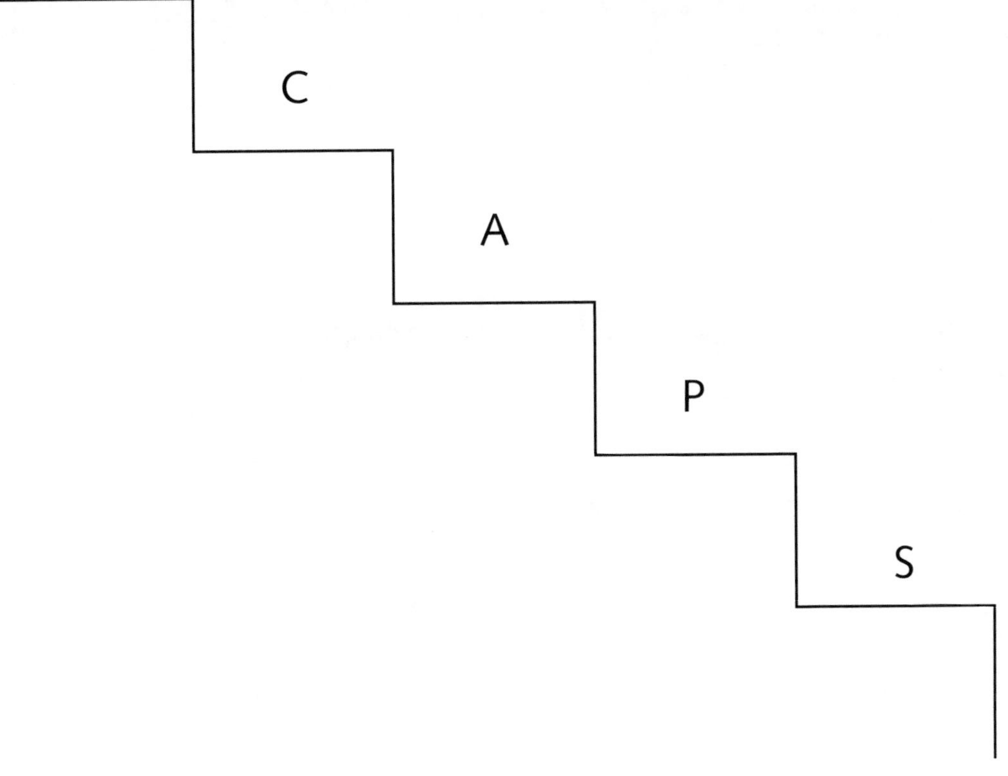


*Maria and Sondra are sisters who are at the top of the escalator. Maria was talking on the telephone to a friend. Sondra kept asking her to get off the phone. After the fourth request, she walked in and hung up the phone on Maria. Now they are yelling at each other.*

Have the students find partners and take two minutes to discuss how Maria and Sondra might use CAPS to come down the escalator. After two minutes, bring the class back together to discuss the conflict as suggested here. As students make suggestions for each step, record their suggestions on the escalator diagram on the board.

Discussion:

- How might Maria and Sondra calm down? (Emphasize that they can still be angry, but they must be reasonably calm in order to discuss the conflict at all.)
- What could they say to each other to agree to work it out? What might be the first thing one of them says?
- How would each girl describe the problem?
- What are some ways they could solve the problem?

Activity A, Handout 1

Date ____________________

Name ____________________________________________

# WHO are we?

Who am *I* in this class?

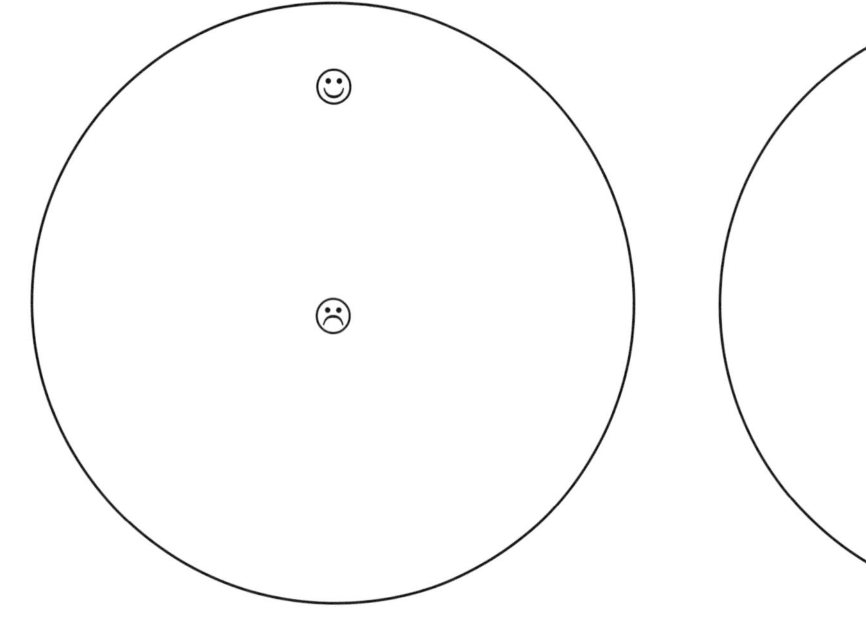

Who are *others* in this class?

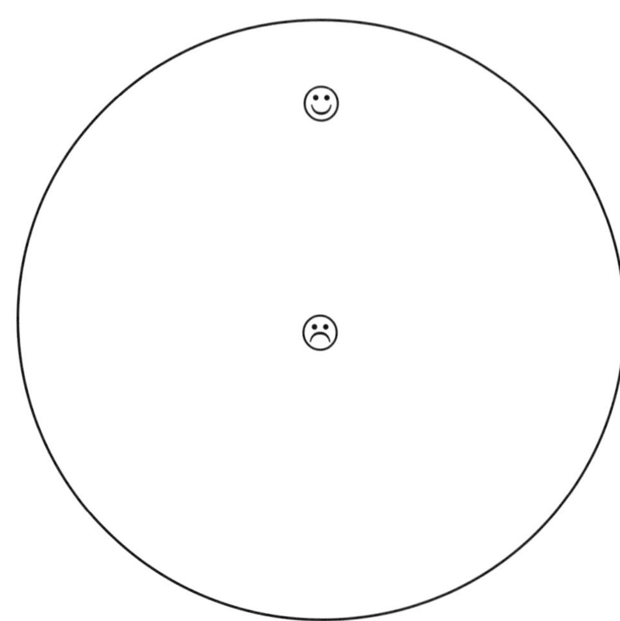

Who are *We*?

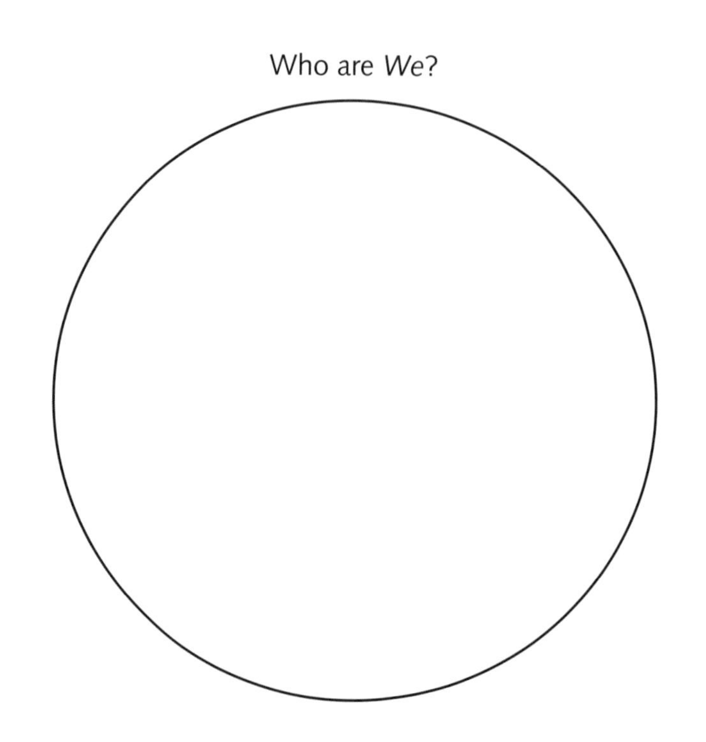

Activity D, Handout 1 Date ____________________

Name ________________________________________________

# active listening practice

**IT'S EASIER FOR OTHERS TO TALK WHEN I...**

- Make good eye contact.
- Assume a nonthreatening distance (not too close, not too distant).
- Am relaxed and show interest in the other person.
- Listen attentively.
- Don't interrupt.
- Paraphrase or restate what the other person is saying to make sure I understand and to make the other person feel heard.
- Ask clarifying questions: "When did this happen?" "Could you explain that?" "What do you mean by that?"
- Encourage the other person to talk: "Can you say more about that?"
- Affirm and reflect the other person's feelings.
- Don't try to solve the problem for the other person.
- Try to see the issue from the other person's perspective.
- Show respect for the other person, even if I disagree.
- Don't give advice, lecture, preach, judge, blame, or criticize.

**IT'S EASIER FOR OTHERS TO LISTEN WHEN I...**

- Exchange facts and information freely.
- Disclose my own feelings and thoughts.
- Don't raise my voice or use an angry or hostile tone.
- Don't use sarcastic language.

Activity E, Handout 1 Date ____________________

Name ____________________________________________________________

# OBSERVATION SHEET
# HOW ARE "WE"?

**Observer's Name** ______________________________

Check (✓) each time a person in the class, at your table, or in your group demonstrates a connecting or disconnecting behavior. Summarize to the group what you have observed without using names.

| **Connecting Behaviors** | |
|---|---|
| Cooperates | |
| Listens | |
| Asks questions | |
| Gives praise | |
| Voices differences with respect | |
| Asks others for ideas | |
| Offers to help out | |
| Clarifies | |
| Other (describe) | |

| **Disconnecting Behaviors** | |
|---|---|
| Interrupts | |
| Bosses | |
| Doesn't listen | |
| Disrupts the task | |
| Puts someone down | |
| Doesn't participate | |
| Doesn't help out | |
| Criticizes | |
| Other (describe) | |

Activity F, Handout 1

Date ____________________

Name ______________________________________________________________

# COMMUNITY SURVEY

**Directions**: For each statement, write a number that represents how you feel about the statement.

| **Item #** | **Measure of Community** | **1=Never 2=Sometimes 3=Often 4=Always** |
|---|---|---|
| 1. | I feel a sense of belonging in this class. | |
| 2. | I value the input and feedback I receive from this class. | |
| 3. | I enjoy the companionship of this class as a whole. | |
| 4. | I feel responsible for the actions of others in this class. | |
| 5. | I feel energized by being part of this class. | |
| 6. | I feel as if I have a better sense of who I am after being in this class. | |
| 7. | I feel better about myself after being in this class. | |
| 8. | I feel like taking positive action (by myself or with others) after being in this class. | |
| 9. | I feel like connecting with other people after being in this class. | |

Activity J, Handout 1

Date ____________________

Name ____________________________________________

# What Makes Conflict Escalate Skits

**Skit A: Tape Player Trouble**

Sharone lent Rachel her portable tape player. Rachel tried three different tapes in it and it chewed up each of them. The next day at school Rachel confronted Sharone.

"Your tape player ruined three of my tapes. You owe me for those tapes," she said.

"What do you mean it ruined your tapes? It never ruined mine. What did you do to it?" Sharone asked.

"I just tried to play my tapes. That tape player is cheap like all the stuff you have. It ruined my favorite tapes."

"I can't believe this. I lent you my tape player because yours was broken and now you're mad at me? I did you a favor!"

"Some favor. Here's your piece of junk," Rachel said, throwing the tape player on Sharone's desk. The tape player fell off the desk and landed on the floor. The cover broke.

"Look what you did. You're going to buy me a new tape player!" Sharone yelled.

"No I'm not! You're going to buy me new tapes!" Rachel yelled back.

**Skit B: Green-Eyed and Grouchy**

James and Darnell have been friends for years, but recently they haven't seen much of each other since Darnell started going with Kindra. James missed hanging out with his friend. He didn't like Kindra that much, but thought that since she and Darnell were definitely a couple, he might as well be friendly towards her. He started going out of his way to be nice to her, talking to her between classes.

One day Darnell confronted him in the hallway. "Don't think I don't know what you're doing," he said angrily.

"What do you mean?" James asked.

"Don't act all innocent with me. I've got eyes. Everyone knows you're coming on to Kindra."

"I was just being friendly," James protested.

"Yeah, sure. You're trying to steal her away. You're just jealous because she's my girlfriend."

"Jealous! You're the one acting like a jealous fool. You're a green-eyed monster. You see things that aren't even there!"

"Man, I thought you were my friend. You've always been jealous of me."

James couldn't stand the superior look Darnell had on his face when he said that. "Jealous of you. There's nothing to be jealous of. You've got nothing I want."

"Well, you'd better stay away from Kindra or you'll be sorry," Darnell warned.

"Like I'm scared of you," James said and walked away.

# TEN STRATEGIES THAT FOSTER CONNECTION TO SCHOOL

*For School Administrators**

1. **Brainstorm** with students, faculty, staff, and parents simple changes that could make school a more pleasant place to be.
2. **Create policies** that are based on student, family, and neighborhood strengths and assets.
3. **Turn mistakes into learning opportunities** rather than failures meriting punishment.
4. **Acknowledge and honor accomplishments** and all types of competencies (such as helpfulness, good citizenship, most improved performance, volunteerism, participation in decision making, and cessation of negative behavior)
5. **Set high standards** and challenge students to meet them.
6. **Reinforce explicit expectations** for positive behavior and academic success.
7. **Encourage** highly interactive teaching strategies.
8. **Create a welcoming environment** for all who come to the school.
9. **Invite family and community members** to take active and regular roles in the daily operation of the school.
10. **Create a common vision** of success and keep it visible.

* *Used with permission from the Center for Adolescent Health and Development, University of Minnesota. Based on material published in "Protective Schools: Linking Drug Abuse Prevention with Student Success," by Kris Bosworth, PhD. Smith Initiatives for Prevention and Education, College of Education, The University of Arizona, Tucson, AZ.*

# TEN STRATEGIES THAT FOSTER CONNECTION TO SCHOOL

*For Parents**

1. **Be a model** of respectful, cooperative, positive behavior in your everyday interactions.
2. **Participate** in school events.
3. **Show interest**. Be involved in your child's academic activities.
4. **Maintain regular contact** with your child's teacher.
5. **Monitor your child's homework** completion and work with him or her on assignments that involve family participation.
6. **Be present** when things go wrong.
7. **Meet** your child's friends, and their parents.
8. **Ask school leaders** what you can do to support them.
9. **Volunteer** at school.
10. **Nominate** effective school leaders for local awards.



** Used with permission from the Center for Adolescent Health and Development, University of Minnesota. Based on material published in "Protective Schools: Linking Drug Abuse Prevention with Student Success," by Kris Bosworth, PhD. Smith Initiatives for Prevention and Education, College of Education, The University of Arizona, Tucson, AZ.*

# TEN STRATEGIES THAT FOSTER CONNECTION TO SCHOOL

*For Teachers**

1. **Help students** get to know each other's (and your) strengths.
2. **Involve students** in planning, problem solving, identifying issues, and assessing curriculum in the classroom.
3. **Promote cooperation** over competition. Post everyone's best work. Offer opportunities for the class to work together to help everyone achieve their level of excellence.
4. **Build a strong relationship** with each student.
5. **Convey attentiveness** to students and excitement about learning through nonverbal gestures.
6. **Involve all students** in chores and responsibilities in the classroom.
7. **Integrate concepts of discipline and respect** for classmates throughout instruction.
8. **Give students more say** in what they will learn.
9. **Involve students** in developing the criteria by which their work will be assessed and provide guidelines so they clearly understand what's expected of them.
10. **Use first person plural** ( we, us, let's) when presenting classroom activities.

* *Used with permission from the Center for Adolescent Health and Development, University of Minnesota. Based on material published in "Protective Schools: Linking Drug Abuse Prevention with Student Success," by Kris Bosworth, PhD. Smith Initiatives for Prevention and Education, College of Education, The University of Arizona, Tucson, AZ.*

# STONE CENTER RESOURCES*

Bergman, S., and Surrey, J. "The Woman-Man Relationship: Impasses and Possibilities." *Work in Progress*, Stone Center Working Paper Series no. 55 (1992).

Bergman, S and Surrey, J. "Couples Therapy: A Relational Approach." *Work in Progress*, Stone Center Working Paper Series no. 66 (1994).

Jordan, J. (ed.), *Women's Growth in Diversity: More Writings from the Stone Center* New York: Guilford, 1997.

Jordan, J., Kaplan, A.G., Miller, J.B., Stiver, I.P., and Surrey, J. *Women's Growth in Connection: Writings from the Stone Center* . New York: Guilford, 1991.

Miller, J.B., and Stiver, I.P. *The Healing Connection: How Women Form Relationships in Therapy and in Life.* Boston, MA: Beacon Press, 1997.

Shem, S. [S. Bergman] and Surrey, J. *We Have to Talk: Healing Dialogues between Women and Men.* New York: Basic Books, 1998.

**The relational/cultural model on which this work is based has been developed at the Jean Baker Miller Training Institute, Stone Center, Wellesley Center for Women at Wellesley College. These publications may be ordered by contacting the Publications Office at 781-283-2510 or through the website: jbmti.org.*

# ENDNOTES

1. Judith Jordan, Alexandra Kaplan, Jean Baker Miller, Irene Stiver, and Janet Surrey, *Women's Growth in Connection: Writings from the Stone Center* (New York: Guilford, 1991); Stephen Bergman, "Men's Psychological Development, a Relational Perspective," *Work in Progress*, Stone Center Working Paper Series, no. 48 (1991); Samuel Shem and Janet Surrey, *We Have to Talk: Healing Dialogues between Women and Men* (New York: Basic Books, 1998).

2. Richard William Blum, Clea McNeeley, and Peggy Mann Rinehardt, *Improving the Odds: The Untapped Power of Schools to Improve the Life of Teens* (Minneapolis: University of Minnesota, Center for Adolescent Health and Development, 2002); Clea McNeeley, Jean Nonnemaker, and Richard William Blum, "Promoting Student Attachment to School: Evidence from the National Longitudinal Study of Adolescent Health," *Journal of School Health* 72, no. 4 (2002); Michael Resnick et al. "Protecting Adolescents from Harm," *Journal of the American Medical Association* 278, no. 10 (1997): 823–32.

3. Blum, McNeeley, and Rinehardt, *Improving the Odds*

4. Jordan et al., *Women's Growth in Connection*.

5. Ibid.

6. Jean Baker Miller and Irene Stiver, *The Healing Connection* (Boston: Beacon Press, 1998).

7. Shem and Surrey, *We Have to Talk*.

8. Nancy Beardall, *Creating a Peaceable School: Confronting Intolerance and Bullying*.(Newton Public Schools: Newton, MA, 2000).

9. See note 3 above.

10. Ibid.

11. Bergman, "Men's Psychological Development"; Shem and Surrey, *We Have to Talk*.

12. Eleanor Macoby, *The Two Sexes: Growing Up Apart, Coming Together* (Cambridge: Harvard University Press, 1998); B. Thorne, *Gender Play: Girls and Boys in School* (New Brunswick: Rutgers University Press, 1994).

13. See note 11 above.

14. Yoko Sugihara and Emiko Katsurada, "Gender Role Development in Japanese Culture: Diminishing Gender Role Differences in a Contemporary Society," *Sex Roles: A Journal of Research* (November 2002).

15. Ellen Bigler, *On Exclusion and Inclusion in Classroom Texts and Talk*, National Research Center on English Learning and Achievement (CELA), Report Series 7.5 (1996), available at http://cela.albany.edu/exin/index.html.

16. See note 14 above.

17. Karen Marcovici, *The UNGASS, Gender and Women's Vulnerability to HIV/AIDS in Latin America and the Caribbean,* Pan-American Health Organization, Regional Office of the World Health Organization, Washington, D.C., December 2002.

18. Kim Schmitz and Sarah Diefenthaler. "An Examination of Traditional Gender Roles Among Men and Women in Mexico and the United States." *Journal of Undergraduate Research University of Wisconsin-La Crosse*. vol 1(1998): 139-143.

19. Ronald Ferguson, *What Doesn't Meet the Eye: Understanding Disparities in High Achieving Suburban Schools,* Weiner Center for Social Policy, John F. Kennedy School of Government, Harvard University, October 21, 2002.

20. Shirley Griggs and Rita Dunn, *Hispanic-American Students and Learning Style,* Clearinghouse on Early Education and Parenting, ERIC/EECE Publications, EDO-PS-96-4, University of Illinois, May 1996.

21. Ibid.

22. Jean Kilbourne, *Deadly Persuasion: Why Women and Girls Must Fight the Addictive Power of Advertising* (New York: Free Press, 1999).

23. Benoit Denizet-Lewis, "Friends, Friends with Benefits, and the Benefits of the Local Mall," *New York Times Magazine*, May 30, 2004.

# ABOUT THE AUTHORS

**Nancy Beardall, ADTR, CMA, LMHC, Ph.D.**, is an educator, dancer, dance/movement therapist, and counselor. Throughout her career, Nancy has been dedicated to bringing dance into the schools. She has also developed social and emotional learning programs through the arts. Nancy has developed the *Creating a Peaceable School: Confronting Intolerance and Bullying,* curriculum which was awarded the Anti-Defamation League's 1998 Teaching Award. She has brought many innovative programs to the Newton Public Schools. At this time Nancy is the coordinator of Newton North's High School Mentors in Violence Prevention program, teaches at Lesley University and has a private practice.

**Stephen Bergman, M.D., Ph.D.**, is a writer, psychiatrist, and educator. He is co-director of the Gender Relations Project at the Stone Center, Wellesley College. With Janet Surrey, he is co-author of the play *Bill W. and Dr. Bob* and *We Have to Talk: Healing Dialogues between Women and Men*. As Samuel Shem, he is author of the novels *The House of God*, *Fine,* and *Mount Misery*. He is also a partner at MPM Capital, a healthcare investment firm.

**Janet Surrey, Ed.M., Ph.D.**, is a clinician, writer and educator. She is a founding scholar of the Jean Baker Miller Training Institute and co-director of the Gender Relations Project at the Stone Center, Wellesley College. She is on the faculty of the Andover-Newton Theological Seminary School and the Institute for Meditation and Psychotherapy. She is co-author of *Women's Growth in Connection*, *Women's Growth in Diversity*, *Mothering Against the Odds*. With Dr. Bergman, she is co-author *We Have to Talk: Healing Dialogues between Women and Men* and the play *Bill W. and Dr. Bob*.

## Contributing Authors

**Gayle Burnett, M.A**, is a writer and consultant in the fields of leadership, diversity and conflict resolution and co-author of *Peace in Everyday Relationships*.

**Lisa Sjostrom, Ed.M.**, is a writer, teacher and program developer who has created curricula on many topics pertaining to children's healthy development. She was the lead writer for Ms. Foundation's "Take Our Daughters to Work" campaign and is co-author of *Flirting or Hurting? Sexual Harassment in School; Bullyproof: A Teacher's Guide on Teasing and Bullying and Full of Ourselves: Advancing Girl Power, Health and Leadership*.